MW00441780

Wagner
on
Conducting

Richard Wagner

TRANSLATED BY EDWARD DANNREUTHER

DOVER PUBLICATIONS, INC., New York

This Dover edition, first published in 1989, is a slightly corrected re-publication of *On Conducting (Ueber das Dirigiren): A Treatise on Style in the Execution of Classical Music*, originally published by William Reeves, London, in 1887.

Manufactured in the United States of America
Dover Publications, Inc., 31 East 2nd Street, Mineola, N.Y. 11501

Library of Congress Cataloging-in-Publication Data

Wagner, Richard, 1813–1883.
    [Über das Dirigieren. English]
    Wagner on conducting / Richard Wagner ; translated by Edward Dannreuther.
          p.   cm.
    Reprint, slightly corr. Originally published: On conducting. London : W. Reeves, 1887.
    ISBN 0-486-25932-3 (pbk.)
    1. Conducting.   I. Title.
ML410.W1A246   1989
781.6'35—dc19   88-26827
                                                     CIP
                                                     MN

(1869).

MOTTO NACH GOETHE:

" Fliegenschnauz' und Mückennas'
  Mit euren Anverwandten,
  Frosch im Laub und Grill' im Gras,
  Ihr seid mir Musikanten ! "

    ⁂ ⁂ ⁂ ⁂ ⁂ ⁂ ⁂ ⁂ ⁂ ⁂

" Flysnout and Midgenose,
  With all your kindred, too.
  Treefrog and Meadow-grig,
  True musicians, *you !* "

(After GOETHE).

The lines travestied are taken from " Oberon und Titanias goldene Hochzeit,'
Intermezzo, Walpurgisnacht.—*Faust* I.

TRANSLATOR'S NOTE.

———o———

Wagner's *Ueber das Dirigiren* was published simultaneously in the "Neue Zeitschrift für Musik" and the "New-Yorker Musik-zeitung," 1869. It was immediately issued in book form, Leipzig, 1869, and is now incorporated in the author's collected writings, Vol. VIII. p. 325—410. (" Gesammelte Schriften und Dichtungen von Richard Wagner," ten volumes, Leipzig, 1871—1883.) For various reasons, chiefly personal, the book met with much opposition in Germany, but it was extensively read, and has done a great deal of good. It is unique in the literature of music : a treatise on style in the execution of classical music, written by a great practical master of the grand style. Certain asperities which pervade it from beginning to end could not well be omitted in the translation ; care has, however, been taken not to exaggerate them. To elucidate some points in the text sundry extracts from other writings of Wagner have been appended. The footnotes, throughout, are the translator's.

THE following pages are intended to form a record of my experience in a department of music which has hitherto been left to professional *routine* and amateur criticism. I shall appeal to professional executants, both instrumentalists and vocalists, rather than to conductors ; since the executants only can tell whether, or not, they have been led by a competent conductor. I do not mean to set up a system, but simply to state certain facts, and record a number of practical observations.

Composers cannot afford to be indifferent to the manner in which their works are presented to the public ; and the public, naturally, cannot be expected to decide whether the performance of a piece of music is correct or faulty, since there are no data beyond the actual effect of the performance to judge by.

I shall endeavour to throw some light upon the characteristics of musical performances in Germany—with regard to the concert-room, as well as to the theatre. Those who have experience in such matters are aware that, in most cases, the defective constitution of German orchestras and the faults of their performances are due to the shortcomings of the conductors (" Capellmeister," " Musikdirectoren," etc.). The demands upon the orchestras have increased greatly of late, their task has become more difficult and more complicated ; yet the directors of our art-institutions, display increasing negligence in their choice of conductors. In the days when Mozart's scores afforded the highest tasks that could be set before an orchestra, the typical German Capellmeister was a formidable personage, who knew how to make himself respected at his post—sure of his business, strict, despotic, and by no means polite. *Friedrich Schneider*, of Dessau, was the last representative I have met with of this now extinct species. *Guhr*, of Frankfort, also may be reckoned as belonging to it. The attitude of these men towards modern music was certainly " old fashioned " ; but, in their own way, they produced good solid work : as I found not more than eight years ago * at Carlsruhe, when old Capellmeister Strauss conducted " Lohengrin." This venerable and worthy man evidently looked at my score with some little shyness ; but, he took good care of the orchestra, which he led with a degree of precision and firmness impossible to excell. He was, clearly, a man not to be trifled with, and his forces obeyed him to perfection. Singularly enough, this old gentleman was the only German conductor of repute I had met with, up to that time, who possessed true fire ; his tempi were more

* Circa, 1861.

often a trifle too quick than too slow ; but they were invariably firm and well marked. Subsequently, H. Esser's conducting, at Vienna, impressed me in like manner.

The older conductors of this stamp if they happened to be less gifted than those mentioned, found it difficult to cope with the complications of modern orchestral music—mainly because of their fixed notions concerning the proper constitution of an orchestra. I am not aware that the number of permanent members of an orchestra, has, in any German town, been rectified according to the requirements of modern instrumentation. Now-a-days, as of old, the principal parts in each group of instruments, are alloted to the players according to the rules of seniority * —thus men take first positions when their powers are on the wane, whilst younger and stronger men are relegated to the subordinate parts—a practice, the evil effects of which are particularly noticeable with regard to the wind instruments. Latterly † by discriminating exertions, and particularly, by the good sense of the instrumentalists concerned, these evils have diminished; another traditional habit, however, regarding the choice of players of stringed instruments, has led to deleterious consequences. Without the slightest compunction, the second violin parts, and especially the Viola parts, have been sacrificed. The viola

---

* Appointments at German Court theatres are usually for life.

† 1869.

is commonly (with rare exceptions indeed) played by infirm violinists, or by decrepit players of wind instruments who happen to have been acquainted with a stringed instrument once upon a time: at best a competent viola player occupies the first desk, so that he may play the occasional soli for that instrument; but, I have even seen this function performed by the leader of the first violins. It was pointed out to me that in a large orchestra, which contained eight violas, there was only one player who could deal with the rather difficult passages in one of my later scores!

Such a state of things may be excusable from a humane point of view; it arose from the older methods of instrumentation, where the rôle of the viola consisted for the most part in filling up the accompaniments; and it has since found some sort of justification in the meagre method of instrumentation adopted by the composers of Italian operas, whose works constitute an important element in the repertoire of the German opera theatres.

At the various court theatres, Italian operas have always found favour with the Directors. From this it follows as a matter of course, that works which are not in the good grace of those gentlemen stand a poor chance, unless it should so happen that the conductor is a man of weight and influence who knows the real requirements of a modern orchestra. But our older Capellmeisters rarely knew as much—they did not choose to recognize the need of a large increase in the number of stringed instruments to balance the augmented number of wind instruments and the complicated uses the latter are now put to.

In this respect the attempts at reform were always insufficient; and our celebrated German orchestras remained far behind those of France in the power and capacity of the violins, and particularly of the violoncellos.

Now, had the conductors of a later generation been men of authority like their predecessors, they might easily have mended matters; but the Directors of court theatres took good care to engage none but demure and subservient persons.

It is well worth while to note how the conductors, who are now at the head of German music, arrived at the honourable positions they hold.

We owe our permanent orchestras to the various theatres, particularly the court theatres, small and great. The managers of these theatres are therefore in a position to select the men who are to represent the spirit and dignity of German music. Perhaps those who have been thus advanced to posts of honour, are themselves cognizant of how they got there—to an unpractised observer it is rather difficult to discern their particular merits. The so-called " good berths " are reached step by step: men move on and push upwards. I believe the Court orchestra at Berlin has got the majority of its conductors in this way. Now and then, however, things come to pass in a more erratic manner; grand personages, hitherto unknown, suddenly begin to flourish under the protection of the lady in waiting to some princess, etc. etc.—It is impossible to estimate the harm done to our leading orchestras and opera theatres by such nonentities. Devoid of real merit they keep their posts by abject cringing to the chief court official, and by polite submission to the indolence of their musical subordinates. Relinquishing the pretence of artistic discipline, which they are unable to enforce, they are always ready to give way, or to obey any absurd orders from headquarters; and such conductors, under favourable circumstances, have even been known to become popular favourites!

At rehearsals all difficulties are got over by means of mutual congratulations and a pious allusion to the "old established fame of our Orchestra." Who can venture to say that the performances of that famous institution deteriorate year by year? Where is the true authority? Certainly not amongst the critics, who only bark when their mouths are not stopped; and the art of stopping mouths is cultivated to perfection.

Recently, the post of chief conductor has here and there been filled by a man of practical experience, especially engaged with a view to stimulating the slumbering energy of his colleagues. Such " chiefs " are famed for their skill in " bringing out" a new opera in a fortnight; for their clever "cuts"; for the effective "closes" they write to please singers, and for their interpolations in other men's scores. Practical accomplishments of this sort have, for instance, supplied the Dresden Opera with one of its most energetic Capellmeisters.

Now and again the managers look out for "a conductor of reputation." Generally none such are to be had at the theatres; but, according to the feuilletons of the political newspapers, the singing societies and concert establishments furnish a steady supply of the article. These are the "music-brokers," as it were, of the present day, who came forth from the school of Mendelssohn, and flourished under his protection and recommendation. They differ widely from the helpless epigonae of our old conductors: they are not musicians brought up in the orchestra or at the theatre, but respectable pupils of the new-fangled conservatoires; composers of Psalms and Oratorios, and devout listeners at rehearsals for the subscription concerts. They have received lessons in conducting too, and are possessed of an elegant "culture" hitherto unknown in the realms of music. Far from shewing any lack of politeness, they managed to transform the timid modesty of our poor native Capellmeister into a sort of cosmopolitan *bon ton*; which stood them in good stead with the old-fashioned philistine society of our towns. I believe the influence of these people upon German orchestras has been good in many respects, and has brought about beneficial results: certainly much that was raw and awkward has disappeared; and, from a musical point of view, many details of refined phrasing and expression are now more

carefully attended to. They feel more at home in the
modern orchestra ; which is indebted to their master—
Mendelssohn—for a particularly delicate and refined
development in the direction opened up by Weber's
original genius.

One thing however is wanting to these gentlemen,
without which they cannot be expected to achieve the
needful reconstruction of the orchestras, nor to enforce
the needful reforms in the institutions connected with
them, *viz.*, energy, self-confidence, and personal power.
In their case, unfortunately, reputation, talent, culture,
even faith, love and hope, are artificial. Each of them
was, and is, so busy with his personal affairs, and the
difficulty of maintaining his artificial position, that he
cannot occupy himself with measures of general
import—measures which might bring about a connected
and consistent new order of things. As a matter of
fact, such an order of things cannot, and does not
concern the fraternity at all. They came to occupy
the position of those old fashioned German masters,
because the power of the latter had deteriorated
and because they had shewn themselves incapable
to meet the wants of a new style ; and it would
appear that they, in their turn, regard their position
of to-day as merely temporary—filling a gap in
a period of transition. In the face of the new
ideals of German art, towards which all that
is noble in the nation begins to turn, they are
evidently at a loss, since these ideals are alien to
their nature. In the presence of certain technical

difficulties inseparable from modern music they
have recourse to singular expedients. Meyerbeer,
for instance, was very circumspect; in Paris he engaged a new flutist and paid him out of his
own pocket to play a particular bit nicely. Fully
aware of the value of finished execution, rich and
independent, Meyerbeer might have been of great
service to the Berlin orchestra when the King of
Prussia appointed him "General Musikdirector."
Mendelssohn was called upon to undertake a similar
mission about the same time; and, assuredly, Mendelssohn was the possessor of the most extraordinary
gifts and attainments. Both men, doubtless, encoun-
tered all the difficulties which had hitherto blocked the
way towards improvements; but they were called upon
to overcome these very difficulties, and their independent position and great attainments rendered them
exceptionally competent to do so. Why then did their
powers desert them? It would seem as if they had no
real power. They left matters to take care of themselves and, now, we are confronted by the "celebrated"
Berlin orchestra in which the last trace of the traditions
of Spontini's strict discipline have faded away. Thus
fared Meyerbeer and Mendelssohn whilst at Berlin:
what are we to expect elsewhere from their neat little
shadows?

It is clear from this account of the survivals of the
earlier and of the latest species of Capellmeisters and
Musikdirectors, that neither of them are likely to do
much towards the reorganization of our orchestras.

On the other hand the initiative has been taken by the orchestral performers themselves; and the signs of progress are evidently owing to the increasing develop-ment of their technical attainments. Virtuosi upon the different orchestral instruments have done excellent service, and they might have done much more in the circumstances had the conductors been competent.

Exceptionally gifted and accomplished players easily got the upper hand of the decrepit Capellmeisters of the old sort, and of their successors, the parvenus without authority—pianoforte pedagogues patronized by ladies in waiting, etc., etc. Virtuosi soon came to play a rôle in the orchestra akin to that of the prima donna on the stage. The elegant con-ductors of the day chose to associate and ally themselves with the virtuosi, and this arrangement might have acted very satisfactorily if the con-ductors had really understood the true spirit of German music.

It is important to point out in this connection that conductors are indebted to the theatres for their posts, and even for the existence of their orchestra. The greater part of their professional work consists in rehearsing and conducting *operas*. They ought, there-fore, to have made it their business to understand the theatre—the opera—and to make themselves masters of the proper application of music to dramatic art, in something like the manner in which an astronomer applies mathematics to astronomy. Had they under-stood dramatic singing and dramatic expression they

might have applied such knowledge to the execution of modern instrumental music.

A long time ago I derived much instruction as to
the tempo and the proper execution of Beethoven's
music from the clearly accentuated and expressive singing of that great artist, Frau Schröder-Devrient. I
have since found it impossible, for example, to permit
the touching cadence of the Oboe in the first movement of the C minor Symphony—

to be played in the customary timid and embarassed
way; indeed, starting from the insight I had gained
into the proper execution of this cadence, I also
found and felt the true significance and expression due

to the sustained fermata of the first violins

in the corresponding place, and from the touching
emotional impressions I got by means of these two
seemingly so insignificant details I gained a new point
of view, from which the entire movement appeared in
a clearer and warmer light.

Leaving this for the present, I am content to point
out that a conductor might exercise great influence

* Ante, bar 21.

upon the higher musical culture with regard to
execution, if he properly understood his position in
relation to dramatic art, to which, in fact, he
is indebted for his post and his dignity. But our
conductors are accustomed to look upon the opera
as an irksome daily task (for which, on the other hand,
the deplorable condition of that genre of art at
German theatres furnishes reason enough); they
consider that the sole source of honour lies in the
concert rooms from which they started and from which
they were called; for, as I have said above, wherever
the managers of a theatre happen to covet a musician
of reputation for Capellmeister, they think themselves
obliged to get him from some place other than a
theatre.

Now to estimate the value of a *quondam* conductor of
concerts and of choral societies at a theatre, it is
advisable to pay him a visit at home, *i.e.*, in the concert-room, from which he derives his reputation as a
"solid" German musician. Let us observe him as a
conductor of orchestral concerts.

LOOKING back upon my earliest youth I remember to have had unpleasant impressions from performances of classical orchestral music. At the piano or whilst reading a score, certain things appeared animated and expressive, whereas, at a performance, they could hardly be recognised, and failed to attract attention. I was puzzled by the apparent flabbiness of Mozartian Melody (Cantilena) which I had been taught to regard as so delicately expressive. Later in life I discovered the reasons for this, and I have discussed them in my report on a "German music school to be established at Munich,"* to which I beg to refer readers who may be interested in the subject. Assuredly, the reasons lie in the want of a proper Conservatorium of German music—a *Conservatory*, in the strictest sense of the word, in which the traditions of the *classical masters' own* style of execution are preserved in practice—which, of course, would imply that the masters should, once at least, have had a chance personally to supervise performances of

---

* " Bericht ueber eine in München zu errichtende deutsche Musikschule " (1865). See Appendix A.

their works in such a place. Unfortunately German culture has missed all such opportunities; and if we now wish to become acquainted with the spirit of a classical composer's music, we must rely on this or that conductor, and upon his notion of what may, or may not, be the proper tempo and style of execution.

In the days of my youth, orchestral pieces at the celebrated Leipzig Gewandhaus Concerts were not conducted at all; they were simply played through under the leadership of Conzertmeister * Mathäi, like overtures and *entr'actes* at a theatre. At least there was no "disturbing individuality," in the shape of a conductor! The principal classical pieces which presented no particular technical difficulties were regularly given every winter; the execution was smooth and precise; and the members of the orchestra evidently enjoyed the annual recurrence of their familiar favourites.

With *Beethoven's Ninth Symphony* alone they could not get on, though it was considered a point of honour to give that work every year. I had copied the score for myself, and made a pianoforte arrange-ment for two hands; but I was so much astonished at the utterly confused and bewildering effect of the Gewandhaus performance that I lost courage, and gave up the study of Beethoven for some time. Later, I found it instructive to note how I came to take true delight in performances of Mozart's instrumental works:

* *i.e.*, the leader of the first violins.

it was when I had a chance to conduct them myself, and
when I could indulge my feelings as to the expressive
rendering of Mozart's cantilena.

I received a good lesson at Paris in 1839, when I
heard the orchestra of the Conservatoire rehearse the
enigmatical Ninth Symphony. The scales fell from my
eyes; I came to understand the value of *correct* execution, and the secret of a good performance. The
orchestra had learnt to look for Beethoven's *melody* in
every bar—that melody which the worthy Leipzig
musicians had failed to discover; and the orchestra
sang that melody. *This was the secret.*

Habeneck, who solved the difficulty, and to whom
the great credit for this performance is due, was not
a conductor of special genius. Whilst rehearsing the
symphony, during an entire winter season, he had
felt it to be incomprehensible and ineffective (would
German conductors have confessed as much?), but
he persisted throughout a second and a third season!
until Beethoven's new *melos* * was understood and
correctly rendered by each member of the orchestra.
Habeneck was a conductor of the old stamp; *he*
was the master—and everyone obeyed him. I cannot
attempt to describe the beauty of this performance.
However, to give an idea of it, I will select a passage
by the aid of which I shall endeavour to shew the
reason why Beethoven is so difficult to render, as well
as the reason for the indifferent success of German
orchestras when confronted by such difficulties. Even

* Melody in all its aspects.

with first class orchestras I have never been able
to get the passage in the first movement

sempre pp

sempre pp

performed with such equable perfection as I then
(thirty years ago) heard it played by the musicians of
the Paris " Orchestre du Conservatoire."* Often in
later life have I recalled this passage, and tried by its
aid to enumerate the desiderata in the execution of
orchestral music : it comprises *movement* and *sustained*
tone, with a *definite degree of power.* † The masterly
execution of this passage by the Paris orchestra consisted in the fact that they played it *exactly* as it is
written.   Neither at Dresden, nor in London ‡ when,

---

* Wagner, however, subsequently admitted that the passage
was rendered to his satisfaction at the memorable performance
of the Ninth Symphony, given May 22nd, 1872, to celebrate the
laying of the foundation stone of the theatre at Bayreuth.

† (" An dieser Stelle ist es mir, bei oft in meinem späteren
Leben erneueter Erinnerung, recht klar geworden, worauf es
beim Orchestervortrag ankommt, weil sie die *Bewegung* und den
gehaltenen Ton, zugleich mit dem Gesetz der *Dynamik* in sich
schliesst.")

‡ Concert of the Philharmonic Society, 26th March, 1855.

in after years, I had occasion to prepare a performance
of the symphony, did I succeed in getting rid of the
annoying irregularity which arises from the change of
bow and change of strings.   Still less could I suppress
an involuntary accentuation as the passage ascends;
musicians, as a rule, are tempted to play an ascending
passage with an increase of tone, and a descending one
with a decrease.   With the fourth bar of the above
passage we invariably got into a crescendo so that
the sustained G flat of the fifth bar was given with
an involuntary yet vehement accent, enough to spoil
the peculiar tonal significance of that note.   The
composer's intention is clearly indicated; but it
remains difficult to prove to a person whose musical
feelings are not of a refined sort, that there is a
great gap between a commonplace reading, and the
reading meant by the composer: no doubt both
readings convey a sense of dissatisfaction, unrest,
longing—but the *quality* of these, the true sense of the
passage, cannot be conveyed unless it is played as the
master imagined it, and as I have not hitherto heard
it given except by the Parisian musicians in 1839.   In
connection with this I am conscious that the impression of dynamical monotony * (if I may risk such an
apparently senseless expression for a difficult phenomenon) together with the unusually varied and ever
irregular movement of intervals in the ascending figure
entering on the prolonged G flat to be sung with such

---

* *i.e.,* a power of tone the degree of which remains unchanged.

infinite delicacy, to which the G natural answers with
equal delicacy, initiated me as by magic to the
incomparable mystery of the spirit.   Keeping my
further practical experience in view, I would ask how
did the musicians of Paris arrive at so perfect a
solution of the difficult problem ?   By the most con-
scientious diligence.   They were not content with
mutual admiration and congratulation (*sich gegenseitig
Complimente zu machen*) nor did they assume that
difficulties must disappear before them as a matter of
course.   French musicians in the main belong to the
Italian school; its influence upon them has been
beneficial in as much as they have thus been taught
to approach music mainly through the medium of the
human voice.   The French idea of playing an instrument well is to be able to *sing* well upon it.   And
(as already said) that superb orchestra *sang* the
symphony.   The possibility of its being well sung
implies that the *true tempo* had been found : and this is
the second point which impressed me at the time.   Old
Habeneck was not the medium of any abstract-
æsthetical inspiration—he was devoid of "genius :"
*but he found the right tempo whilst persistently fixing the
attention of his orchestra upon the* MELOS * *of the
symphony.*

The right comprehension of the MELOS *is the sole guide
to the right tempo;* these two things are inseparable: the
one implies and qualifies the other.

---

* *Melody* in all its aspects.

As a proof of my assertion that the majority of performances of instrumental music with us are faulty it is sufficient to point out that *our conductors so frequently fail to find the true tempo because they are ignorant of singing*. I have not yet met with a German Capellmeister or Musik-director who, be it with good or bad voice, can really sing a melody. These people look upon music as a singularly abstract sort of thing, an amalgam of grammar, arithmetic, and digital gymnastics;—to be an adept in which may fit a man for a mastership at a conservatory or a musical gymnasium ; but it does not follow from this that he will be able to put life and soul into a musical performance.

THE whole duty of a conductor is comprised in his ability always to indicate the right *tempo*. His choice of tempi will show whether he understands the piece or not. With good players again the true tempo induces correct phrasing and expression, and conversely, with a conductor, the idea of appropriate phrasing and expression will induce the conception of the true tempo.

This, however, is by no means so simple a matter as it appears. Older composers probably felt so, for they are content with the simplest general indications. Haydn and Mozart made use of the term " Andante " as the mean between " Allegro " and " Adagio," and thought it sufficient to indicate a few gradations and modifications of these terms.

Sebastian Bach, as a rule, does not indicate tempo at all, which in a truly musical sense is perhaps best. He may have said to himself : whoever does not understand my themes and figures, and does not feel their character and expression, will not be much the wiser for an Italian indication of tempo.

Let me be permitted to mention a few facts which

concern me personally. In my earlier operas I gave detailed directions as to the tempi, and indicated them (as I thought) accurately, by means of the Metronome. Subsequently, whenever I had occasion to protest against a particularly absurd tempo, in Tannhäuser for instance, I was assured that the Metronome had been consulted and carefully followed. In my later works I omitted the metronome and merely described the main tempi in general terms, paying, however, particular attention to the various modifications of tempo. It would appear that general directions also tend to vex and confuse Capellmeisters, especially when they are expressed in plain German words. Accustomed to the conventional Italian terms these gentlemen are apt to lose their wits when, for instance, I write "moderate." Not long ago a Capellmeister complained of that term (mässig) which I employed in the score of "Das Rheingold"; the music, (it was reported) lasted exactly two hours and a half at rehearsals under a conductor whom I had personally instructed; whereas, at the performances and under the beat of the official Capellmeister, it lasted fully three hours! (according to the report of the *Allgemeine Zeitung*). Wherefore, indeed, did I write "Mässig"? To match this I have been informed that the overture to Tannhäuser, which, when I conducted it at Dresden, used to last twelve minutes, now lasts twenty. No doubt I am here alluding to thoroughly incompetent persons who are particularly shy of *Alla breve* time, and who stick to their correct

and normal crotchet beats, four in a bar, merely to
shew they are present and conscious of doing something. Heaven knows how such " quadrupeds " find
their way from the village church to our opera theatres.
But " dragging " is not a characteristic of the elegant
conductors of these latter days ; on the contrary
they have a fatal tendency to hurry and to run away
with the tempi. *This tendency to hurry* is so characteristic a mark of our entire musical life latterly, that I
propose to enter into some details with regard to it.

Robert Schumann once complained to me at Dresden
that he could not enjoy the Ninth Symphony at the
Leipzig Gewandhaus concerts because of the quick
tempi *Mendelssohn* chose to take, particularly in the
first movement. I have, myself, only once been present
at a rehearsal of one of Beethoven's Symphonies, when
Mendelssohn conducted ; the rehearsal took place at
Berlin, and the Symphony was No. 8 (in F major). I
noticed that he chose a detail here and there—almost
at random—and worked at it with a certain obstinacy,
until it stood forth clearly. This was so manifestly to
the advantage of the detail that I could not but
wonder why he did not take similar pains with other
nuances. For the rest, this incomparably bright
symphony was rendered in a remarkably smooth and
genial manner. Mendelssohn himself once re-
marked to me, with regard to conducting, that he
thought most harm was done by taking a tempo too
slow ; and that on the contrary, he always recommended quick tempi as being less detrimental. Really

good execution, he thought, was at all times a rare thing, but short-comings might be disguised if care was taken that they should not appear very prominent ; and the best way to do this was "to get over the ground quickly." This can hardly have been a casual view, accidentally mentioned in conversation. The master's pupils must have received further and more detailed instruction ; for, subsequently, I have, on various occasions, noticed the consequences of that maxim "take quick tempi," and have, I think, discovered the reasons which may have led to its adoption.

I remembered it well, when I came to lead the orchestra of the Philharmonic Society in London, 1855. Mendelssohn had conducted the concerts during several seasons, and the tradition of his readings was carefully preserved. It appears likely that the habits and peculiarities of the Philharmonic Society suggested to Mendelssohn his favourite style of performance (Vortragsweise)—certainly it was admirably adapted to meet their wants. An unusual amount of instrumental music is consumed at these concerts ; but, as a rule, each piece is rehearsed once only. Thus in many instances, I could not avoid letting the orchestra follow its traditions, and so I became acquainted with a style of performance which called up a lively recollection of Mendelssohn's remarks.

The music gushed forth like water from a fountain ; there was no arresting it, and every Allegro ended as an undeniable Presto. It was troublesome and difficult to interfere ; for when correct tempi and proper modifications of these were taken the defects of style which the flood had carried along or concealed became painfully apparent. The orchestra generally played *mezzoforte* ; no real *forte*, no real *piano* was attained. Of course, in important cases I took care to enforce the reading I thought the true one, and to insist upon the right tempo. The excellent musicians did not object to this ; on the contrary, they showed themselves sincerely glad of it; the public also approved, but the critics were annoyed and continued so to browbeat the directors of the society that the latter actually requested me to permit the second movement of Mozart's Symphony in E flat to be played in the flabby and colourless way (*ruschlich herunter spielen*) they had been accustomed to—and which, they said, even Mendelssohn himself had sanctioned.

The fatal maxims came to the front quite clearly when I was about to rehearse a symphony by a very amiable elderly contrapuntist, Mr. Potter, * if I mistake not. The composer approached me in a pleasant way, and asked me to take the Andante rather quickly as he feared it might prove tedious. I assured him that his Andante, no matter how short its duration might be, would inevitably prove tedious if it was played in a vapid and inexpressive manner ; whereas if the orchestra could be got to play the very pretty and ingenious theme, as I felt confident he meant it and as

* Cipriani Potter, 1792-1871, pianist and composer, author of " Recollections of Beethoven." etc.

I now sang it to him, it would certainly please. Mr. Potter was touched ; he agreed, and excused himself, saying that latterly he had not been in the habit of reckoning upon this sort of orchestral playing. In the evening, after the Andante, he joyfully pressed my hand.

I have often been astonished at the singularly slight sense for tempo and execution evinced by leading musicians. I found it impossible, for instance, to communicate to Mendelssohn what I felt to be a perverse piece of negligence with regard to the tempo of the third movement in Beethoven's Symphony in F major, No. 8. This is one of the instances I have chosen out of many to throw light upon certain dubious aspects of music amongst us.

We know that Haydn in his principal later symphonies used the form of the *Menuet* as a pleasant link between the Adagio and the final Allegro, and that he thus was induced to increase the speed of the movement considerably, contrary to the character of the true *Menuet*. It is clear that he incorporated the " Ländler," * particularly in the " Trio "—so that, with regard to the tempo, the designation " Menuetto " is hardly appropriate, and was retained for conventional reasons only. Nevertheless, I believe Haydn's Menuets are generally taken too quick ; undoubtedly the Menuets of Mozart's Symphonies are ; this will be felt very distinctly if, for instance, the

---

* A South German country dance in $\frac{3}{4}$ time, from which the modern waltz is derived.

Menuetto in Mozart's Symphony in G minor, and still
more that of his Symphony in C major, be played a
little slower than at the customary pace. It will be
found that the latter Menuet, which is usually hurried,
and treated almost as a Presto, will now shew an
amiable, firm and festive character; in contrast
with which, the trio, with its delicately sustained

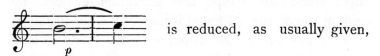 is reduced, as usually given,

to an empty hurry-skurry (eine nichtssagende
Nuschelei). Now Beethoven, as is not uncommon
with him, meant to write a true Menuet in his F major
Symphony; he places it between the two main Allegro
movements as a sort of complementary antithesis (ein
gewissermassen ergänzender Gegensatz) to an *Allegretto
scherzando* which precedes it, and to remove any doubt
as to his intentions regarding the Tempo he designates
it *not* as a Menuetto : but as a *Tempo di Menuetto.*
This novel and unconventional characterization of the
two middle movements of a symphony was almost
entirely overlooked : the *Allegretto scherzando* was taken
to represent the usual Andante, the *Tempo di Menuetto,*
the familiar " Scherzo " and, as the two movements
thus interpreted seemed rather paltry, and none of the
usual effects could be got with them, our musicians
came to regard the entire symphony as a sort of
accidental *hors d'œuvre* of Beethoven's muse—who,
after the exertions with the A major symphony had

chosen "to take things rather easily." Accordingly
after the Allegretto Scherzando, the time of which is invariably "dragged" somewhat, the Tempo di Minuetto
is universally served up as a refreshing "Ländler,"
which passes the ear without leaving any distinct
impression. Generally, however, one is glad when the
tortures of the *Trio* are over. This loveliest of idylls is
turned into a veritable monstrosity by the passage
in triplets for the violoncello; which, if taken at the
usual quick pace, is the despair of violoncellists, who
are worried with the hasty staccato across the strings
and back again, and find it impossible to produce
anything but a painful series of scratches. Naturally,
this difficulty disappears as soon as the delicate
melody of the horns and clarinets is taken at the
proper tempo; these instruments are thus relieved
from the special difficulties pertaining to them, and
which, particularly with the clarinet, at times render it
likely to produce a "quack" * even in the hands of
skilful players. I remember an occasion when all
the musicians began to breathe at ease on my taking
this piece at the true moderate pace: then the
humorous *sforzato* of the basses and bassoons

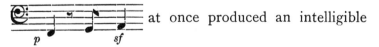 at once produced an intelligible

effect; the short *crescendi* became clear, the delicate
pianissimo close was effective, and the gentle gravity of

---

* *Anglice*, "a goose,"

the returning principal movement was properly felt. Now, the late Capellmeister Reissiger, of Dresden, once conducted this symphony there, and I happened to be present at the performance together with Mendelssohn; we talked about the dilemma just described, and its proper solution; concerning which I told Mendelssohn that I believed I had convinced Reissiger, who had promised that he would take the tempo slower than usual. Mendelssohn perfectly agreed with me. We listened. The third movement began and I was terrified on hearing precisely the old Ländler tempo; but before I could give vent to my annoyance Mendelssohn smiled, and pleasantly nodded his head, as if to say "now it's all right! Bravo!" So my terror changed to astonishment. Reissiger, for reasons which I shall discuss presently, may not have been so very much to blame for persisting in the old tempo; but Mendelssohn's indifference, with regard to this queer artistic *contretemps*, raised doubts in my mind whether he saw any distinction and difference in the case at all. I fancied myself standing before an abyss of superficiality, a veritable void.

Soon after this had happened with Reissiger, the very same thing took place with the same movement of the Eighth Symphony at Leipzig. The conductor, in the latter case, was a well-known successor of Mendelssohn at the Gewandhaus concerts. * He also had agreed with my views as to the *Tempo di Menuetto*, and had invited me to attend a concert at which he promised to take it at the proper moderato pace. He did not keep his word and offered a queer excuse : he laughed, and confessed that he had been disturbed with all manner of administrative business, and had only remembered his promise after the piece had begun ; naturally he could not then alter the tempo, etc. The explanation was sufficiently annoying. Still I could, at least, flatter myself that I had found somebody to share my views as to the difference between one tempo and another.   I doubt, however, whether the conductor could be fairly reproached with a want of forethought and consideration ; unconsciously, perhaps, he may have had a very good reason for his " forgetfulness." It would have been very indiscreet to risk a change of tempo which had not been rehearsed.   For the

* Ferdinand Hiller.

orchestra, accustomed to play the piece in a quick
tempo, would have been disturbed by the sudden
imposition of a more moderate pace; which, as a
matter of course, demands a totally different style of
playing.

We have now reached an important and decisive
point, an appreciation of which is indispensable if we
care to arrive at a satisfactory conclusion regarding the
execution of classical music.   Injudicious tempi might
be defended with some show of reason inasmuch as a
factitious style of delivery has arisen in conformity
with them, and to the uninitiated such conformity of
style and tempo might appear as a proof that all was
right.   The evil, however, is apparent enough if only
the right tempo is taken, in which case the false style
becomes quite unbearable.

To illustrate this, in the simplest possible way,
let us take the opening of the C minor Symphony

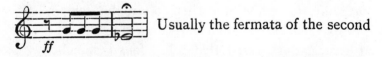 Usually the fermata of the second

bar is left after a slight rest; our conductors hardly
make use of this fermata for anything else than to fix
the attention of their men upon the attack of the figure
in the third bar.   In most cases the note E flat is not
held any longer than a forte produced with a careless
stroke of the bow will last upon the stringed instruments.   Now, suppose the voice of Beethoven were
heard from the grave admonishing a conductor:

" Hold my fermata firmly, terribly! I did not write fermatas in jest, or because I was at a loss how to proceed; I indulge in the fullest, the most sustained tone to express emotions in my Adagio; and I use this full and firm tone when I want it in a passionate Allegro as a rapturous or terrible spasm. Then the very life blood of the tone shall be extracted to the last drop. I arrest the waves of the sea, and the depths shall be visible; or, I stem the clouds, disperse the mist, and show the pure blue ether and the glorious eye of the sun. For this I put *fermatas*, sudden long-sustained notes in my Allegro. And now look at my clear thematic intention with the sustained E flat after the three stormy notes, and understand what I meant to say with other such sustained notes in the sequel." * Suppose a conductor were to

* In the orignal this fine passage is: " Nun setzen wir den Fall, die Stimme Beethoven's habe aus den Grabe einem Dirigenten zugerufen; Halte du meine Fermate lange und furchtbar! Ich schrieb keine Fermaten zum Spass oder aus Verlegenheit, etwa um mich auf das Weitere zu besinnen; sondern, was in meinem Adagio der ganz und voll aufzusaugende Ton für den Ausdruck der schwelgenden Empfindung ist, dasselbe werfe ich, wenn ich es brauche, in das heftig und schnell figurirte Allegro, als wonnig oder schrecklich anhaltenden Krampf. Dann soll das Leben des Tones bis auf seinen letzten Blutstropfen aufgesogen werden; dann halte ich die Wellen meines Meeres an, und lasse in seinen Abgrund blicken; oder hemme ich den Zug der Wolken, zertheile die wirren Nebelstreifen, und lasse einmal in den reinen blauen Aether, in das strahlende Auge der Sonne schauen. Hierfür setze ich Fermaten, d. h. plötzlich eintretende lang auszuhaltende Noten in meine Allegro's. Und nun beachte du, welche ganz bestimmte thematische Absicht ich mit diesem ausgehaltenen Es nach drei stürmisch kurzen Noten hatte, und was ich mit allen den im Folgenden gleich auszuhaltenden Noten gesagt haben will."

attempt to hold the fermata as here directed, what would be the result ? A miserable failure. After the initial power of the bow of the stringed instruments had been wasted, their tone would become thin and thinner, ending in a week and timid piano : for—(and here is one of the results of indifferent conducting)— our orchestras now-a-days hardly know what is meant by *equally sustained tone*. Let any conductor ask any orchestral instrument, no matter which, for a full and prolonged *forte*, and he will find the player puzzled, and will be astonished at the trouble it takes to get what he asks for.

Yet *tone sustained with equal power* is the basis of all expression, * with the voice as with the orchestra : the manifold modifications of the power of tone, which constitute one of the principal elements of musical expression, rest upon it. Without such basis an orchestra will produce much noise but no power. And this is one of the first symptoms of the weakness of most of our orchestral performances. The conductors of the day care little about a sustained forte, but they are particularly fond of an *exaggerated piano*. Now the strings produce the latter with ease, but the wind instruments, particularly the wood winds do not. It is almost impossible to get a delicately sustained piano from wind instruments.

The players, flautists particularly, have transformed their formerly delicate instruments into formidable

* *Die Basis aller Dynamik.*

tubes (Gewaltsröhren). French oboists, who have preserved the pastoral character of their instrument, and our clarinetists, when they make use of the " Echo effect," are the exceptions.

This drawback, which exists in our best orchestras, suggests the question : why, at least, do not conductors try to equalise matters by demanding a somewhat fuller piano from the strings? But the conductors do not seem to notice any discrepancy.

To a considerable extent the fault lies not so much with the wind instruments, as in the character of the *piano* of the strings; for we do not possess a *true piano*, just as we do not possess a *true forte ;* both are wanting in fulness of tone—to attain which our stringed instruments should watch the tone of the winds. Of course it is easy enough to produce a buzzing vibration by gently passing the bow over the strings; but it requires great artistic command of the breath to produce a delicate and pure tone upon a wind instrument. Players of stringed instruments should copy the full-toned piano of the best winds, and the latter, again, should endeavour to imitate the best vocalists.

The sustained soft tone here spoken of, and the sustained powerful tone mentioned above, are the two poles of orchestral expression.*

But what about orchestral execution if neither the one nor the other is properly forthcoming? Where

---

* *Dynamik des Orchesters.*

are the modifications of expression to come from if
the very means of expression are defective? Thus,
the Mendelssohnian rule of "getting over the
ground" (*des flotten Darüberhinweggehens*) suggested
a happy expedient ; conductors gladly adopted the
maxim, and turned it into a veritable dogma ; so that,
nowadays, attempts to perform classical music correctly
are openly denounced as heretical!

I am persistently returning to the question of
tempo because, as I said above, this is the point at
which it becomes evident whether a conductor understands his business or not.

Obviously the proper pace of a piece of music is
determined by the particular character of the rendering it requires ; the question, therefore, comes to this :
does the sustained tone, the vocal element, the
cantilena predominate, or the rhythmical movement? (Figuration). The conductor should lead
accordingly.

The *Adagio* stands to the *Allegro* as the sustained
tone stands to the *rhythmical movement* (*figurirte
Bewegung*). The sustained tone regulates the *Tempo
Adagio :* here the rhythm is as it were dissolved in
pure tone, the tone *per se* suffices for the musical
expression. In a certain delicate sense it may be said
of the pure Adagio that it cannot be taken too slow.
A rapt confidence in the sufficiency of pure musical
speech should reign here ; the *languor* of feeling grows
to ecstasy; that which in the Allegro was expressed
by changes of figuration, is now conveyed by means of

variously inflected tone. Thus the least change of harmony may call forth a sense of surprise ; and again, the most remote harmonic progressions prove accept-able to our expectant feelings.

None of our conductors are courageous enough to take an Adagio in this manner; they always begin by looking for some bit of figuration, and arrange their tempo to match. I am, perhaps, the only conductor who has ventured to take the Adagio section of the third movement of the Ninth Symphony at the pace proper to its peculiar character. This character is distinctly contrasted with that of the alternating *Andante* in triple time; but our conductors invariably contrive to obliterate the difference, leaving only the rhythmical change between square and triple time. This movement (assuredly one of the most instructive in the present respect), finally (in the section in twelve-eight time), offers a conspicuous example of the breaking up of the pure Adagio by the more marked rhythms of an in-dependent accompaniment, during which the cantilena is steadily and broadly continued. In this section we may recognize, as it were, a fixed and consoli-dated reflex* of the Adagio's tendency towards in-

---

* In the original : " Hier erkennen wir das gleichsam fixirte Bild des zuvor nach unendlicher Ausdehnung verlangenden Adagio's, und wie dort eine uneingeschränkte Freiheit für die Befriedigung des tonischen Ausdruckes das zwischen zartesten Gesetzen schwankende Maass der Bewegung angab, wird hier durch die feste Rhythmik der figurativ geschmückten Begleitung das neue Gesetz der Festhaltung einer bestimmten Bewegung gegeben, welches in seinen ausgebildeten Konsequenzen uns zum Gesetz für das Zeitmaass des Allegro wird."

finite expansion; there, limitless freedom in the
expression of sound, with fluctuating, yet delicately
regulated movement; here, the firm rhythm of the
figurated accompaniments, imposing the new regula-
tion of a steady and distinct pace—in the consequences
of which, when fully developed, we have got the law
that regulates the movement of the *Allegro* in general.

We have seen that sustained tone with its modifications is the basis of all musical execution. Similarly
the Adagio, developed, as Beethoven has developed it
in the third movement of his Ninth Symphony, may be
taken as the basis of all regulations as to musical time.
In a certain delicate sense the Allegro may be
regarded as the final result of a refraction (Brechung)
of the pure Adagio-character by the more restless
moving figuration. On careful examination of the
principal motives of the Allegro it will be found that
the melody (Gesang) derived from the Adagio, pre-
dominates. The most important Allegro movements
of Beethoven are ruled by a predominant melody
which exhibits some of the characteristics of the
Adagio; and in this wise Beethoven's Allegros receive
the *emotional sentimental* significance which distin-
guishes them from the earlier *naïve* species of Allegro.
However, Beethoven's*

* Symphony III. " Eroica."

and Mozart's*

or :—

are not far asunder. And with Mozart, as with
Beethoven, the exclusive character of the Allegro is
only felt when the figuration gets the upper hand of
the melody (Gesang) that is, when the reaction of the
rhythmical movement against the sustained tone is
entirely carried out. This is particularly the case in
those final movements which have grown out of the
Rondeau, and of which the Finales to Mozart's
Symphony in E flat, and to Beethoven's in A, are
excellent examples. Here the purely rhythmical movement, so to speak, celebrates its orgies; and it is
consequently impossible to take these movements too
quick. But whatever lies between these two extremes
*is subject to the laws of mutual relationship and interdepen-
dence; and such laws cannot be too delicately and variously
applied,* for they are fundamentally identical with the

* Symphony in C major, "Jupiter."

laws which modify all conceivable *nuances* of the sustained tone.

I shall now turn to the question of the *modification of Tempo*; a question of which our conductors know nothing, and for which they consequently profess contempt. Whoever has followed me so far with attention will, I trust, understand that this question goes to the root of the matter before us.

In the course of the argument so far, two species of Allegro have been mentioned ; an emotional and sentimental character has been assigned to the latter, the true Beethovenian Allegro, whereas the older Mozartian Allegro was distinguished as showing a naïve character. I have adopted the expressions "sentimental" and "naïve" from Schiller's well-known essay upon " sentimental and naïve poetry."

It is needless to discuss the æsthetic problems Schiller touches upon. It is enough to state here that I take Mozart's quick Alla-breve movements as representative of the *naïve* Allegro. The Allegros of the overtures to his operas, particularly to " Figaro " and " Don Giovanni " are the most perfect specimens. It is well known that Mozart wished these pieces to be played as fast as possible. Having driven his musicians into a sort of rage, so that to their own surprise they successfully rendered the unheard of Presto of his overture to " Figaro," he commended them, saying : " that was beautiful ! Let us take it still quicker this evening." Quite right. As I have said of the pure Adagio that, in an ideal sense, it cannot be taken too slowly, so this pure unmixed Allegro cannot be given too quickly.

The slow emanations of pure tone on the one hand, and the most rapid figurated movement on the other, are subject to ideal limits only, and in both directions the law of beauty is the sole measure of what is possible. The law of beauty establishes the point of contact at which the opposite extremes tend to meet and to unite. The order of the movements in the symphonies of our masters—from the opening Allegro, to the Adagio, and thence by means of a stricter dance-form (the Menuet or Scherzo), to the quickest Allegro (Finale)—shows a perfect sense of fitness. To my mind, however, there are signs of a deterioration of the sense of fitness when composers exhibit their platitudes in the *Suite*,* and attempt to bolster up that old form, with its less thoughtfully arranged succession of typical dance tunes; for these have been fully developed elsewhere, and have already been embodied in far richer, more extensive and complex forms.

Mozart's *absolute* Allegros belong to the *naïve* species. As regards the various degrees of power of tone (*Nach der Seite der Dynamik hin*) they consist of simple changes of *piano* and *forte*; and, as regards structure they show certain fixed and stable rhythmic melodic traits (*Formen*) which, without much choice or sifting, are placed side by side, and made to chime with the changes of *piano* and *forte;* and which (in the bustling ever-recurring semi-cadences) the

---

*Compare Franz Lachner's Suites for Orchestra.

master employs with more than surprising ease. But such things—even the greatest negligence (*Achtlosigkeit*) in the use of common-place phrases and sections—are explicable and excusable from the nature of this sort of Allegro, which is not meant to interest by means of Cantilena, but in which the restless incessant movement is intended to produce a certain excitement. It is a significant trait in the Allegro of the overture to Don Giovanni that this restless movement ends with an unmistakable turn towards the "sentimental." Here—where the extremes meet, at the point of contact indicated above—it becomes necessary to modify the tempo in the bars leading from the overture to the first tempo of the opera (which is also an alla-breve but a slower one)—and the pace must be slackened accordingly. But our conductors, in their customary crude way, generally miss this point in the overture. We need not, however, now be lead into premature reflections. Let us merely consider it established that the character of the older classical or, as I call it, *naïve* Allegro differs greatly from the new emotional sentimental Allegro, peculiar to Beethoven. Mozart became acquainted with the orchestral *crescendo* and *diminuendo* at Mannheim, (in 1777) when the orchestra there had acquired it as a novelty: up to that time the instrumentation of the old masters shows that, as a rule, nothing was inserted between the forte and piano sections of the allegro movements which can have been intended to be played with emotional expression.

Now, how does the true Beethovenian Allegro appear
with regard to this? To take the boldest and most
inspired example of Beethoven's unheard-of innova-
tion in this direction, the first movement of his
Sinfonia eroïca : how does this movement appear if
played in the strict tempo of one of the Allegros of
Mozart's overtures? But do our conductors ever dream
of taking it otherwise ? Do they not always proceed
monotonously from the first bar to the last ? With
the members of the " elegant " tribe of Capellmeisters
the " conception " of the tempo consists of an application of the Mendelssohnian maxim " *chi va presto va
sano.*"

Let the players who happen to have any regard
for proper execution make the best of it in passages
like :—

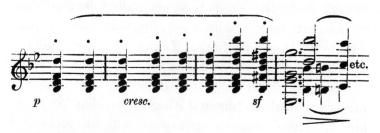

or the plaintive :—

the conductors do not trouble their minds about
such details ; they are on " classic ground," and will

not stop for trifles; they prefer to progress rapidly
"*grande vitesse*," "time is money."

We have now reached the point in our discussion
from which we can judge the music of the day. It
will have been noticed that I have approached this
point with some circumspection. I was anxious to
expose the dilemma, and to make everyone see and
feel that since Beethoven there has been a very considerable change in the treatment and the execution of
instrumental music. Things which formerly existed in
separate and opposite forms, each complete in itself, are
now placed in juxtaposition, and further developed, one
from the other, so as to form a whole. It is essential
that the style of execution shall agree with the matter
set forth—that the tempo shall be imbued with life as
delicate as the life of the thematic tissue. We may
consider it established that in classical music written
in the later style *modification* of Tempo is a *sine qua non*.
No doubt very great difficulties will have to be overcome. Summing up my experiences I do not hesitate
to assert that, as far as public performances go, Beethoven is still a pure chimera with us. *

I shall now attempt to describe what I conceive to
be the right way of performing Beethoven, and music
akin to his. In this respect also the subject seems
inexhaustible, and I shall again confine myself to a few
salient points.

One of the principal musical forms consists of a
series of *Variations* upon a theme. Haydn, and

* *i.e.*, in 1869.

eventually Beethoven, have improved this form, and rendered it artistically significant, by the originality of their devices, and particularly, by connecting the single variations one with the other, and establishing relations of mutual dependance between them. This is accomplished with the happiest results in cases where one variation is developed from another—that is to say, when a degree of movement, suggested in the one is carried further in the other, or when a certain satisfactory sense of surprise is occasioned by one variation supplying a complementary form of movement, which was wanting in the one before it. The real weakness of the Variation-form, however, becomes apparent when strongly contrasting parts are placed in juxtaposition, without any link to connect them. Beethoven often contrives to convert this same weakness into a source of strength ; and he manages to do so in a manner which excludes all sense of accident or of awkwardness: namely—at the point which I have described above as marking the limits of the laws of beauty with regard to the sustained tone (in the Adagio), and the unfettered movement (in the Allegro)— he contrives to satisfy, in a seemingly abrupt way, the extreme longing after an antithesis; which antithesis, by means of a different and contrasting movement, is now made to serve as a relief. This can be observed in the master's greatest works. The last movement of the *Sinfonia eroïca*, for instance, affords excellent instruction in this respect; it should be understood as a movement consisting of a greatly expanded series of variations ; and accordingly it should be interpreted with as much variety as possible. To do this properly, here as in all similar cases, the above mentioned weakness of the Variation-form, and the disadvantage which is felt to result from it, must be taken into account. Single and separate variations are frequently seen to have had each an independent origin, and to have merely been strung together in a conventional manner. The unpleasant effects of such fortuitous juxtaposition are particularly felt in cases where a quiet and sustained theme is followed by an exceptionally lively variation.

The first variation on that most wonderful theme in Beethoven's grand Sonata in A major for piano and violin (Kreutzer) is an example. Virtuosi always treat this as "a first variation" of the common type—*i.e.*, a mere display of musical gymnastics, which destroys all desire to listen any further. It is curious that, whenever I have mentioned the case of this variation to anyone, my experience with the *tempo di minuetto* of the eighth symphony has been repeated. Everybody agreed with me "on the whole"; but in particular, people failed to see what I was aiming at. Certainly (to go on with the example) this first variation of that lovely sustained theme is of a conspicuously lively character; when the composer invented it he could hardly have thought of it as immediately following the theme, or as being in direct contact with it. The component parts of the Variation-form are each complete in themselves, and perhaps the composer was unconsciously influenced by this fact. But, when the entire piece is played, the parts appear in uninterrupted succession. We know from other movements of the master's (for instance the second movement of the C minor symphony, the Adagio of the great quartet in E flat, and above all from the wonderful second movement of the great sonata in C minor, Op. 111), which are all written in the form of Variations, but in which the parts are conceived as standing in immediate connection, how deftly and delicately the links between the different variations can be contrived. A player who, in a case like that of the so-called "Kreutzer-Sonata," claims the honour of representing the master in full, might, at least, attempt to establish some sort of relation and connection between the sentiment of the theme and that of the first variation ; he might begin the latter at a more moderate pace, and gradually lead up to the lively movement. Pianoforte and violin players are firmly persuaded that the character of this variation differs considerably from that of the theme. Let them then interpret it with artistic discrimination, and treat the first part of the variation as a gradual approach to the new tempo; thus adding a charm to the interest the part already possesses *per se*.

A stronger case, of similar import, will be found in the beginning of the first Allegro 6-8 after the long introductory Adagio of the string quartet in C sharp minor. * This is marked "*molto vivace*," and the

* Op. 131.

character of the entire movement is thus appropriately
indicated. In quite an exceptional way, however,
Beethoven has, in this quartet, so arranged the several
movements that they are heard in immediate succession, without the customary interval; indeed they
appear to be developed one from the other according
to certain delicate laws. Thus the Allegro immediately
follows an Adagio full of a dreamy sadness, not to be
matched elsewhere in the master's works. If it
were permitted to interpret the Allegro as showing a
state of feeling, such as could in some sort be
reproduced in pictorial language, (*deutbares Stim-
mungsbild*) one might say that it shews a most
lovely phenomenon, which arises, as it were, from
the depths of memory, and which, as soon as it
has been apprehended, is warmly taken up, and
cherished. Evidently the question, with regard to
execution, here is: how can this phenomenon
(the new Allegro theme) be made to arise
naturally from the sad and sombre close of the Adagio,
so that its abrupt appearance shall prove attractive
rather than repellant? Very appropriately, the new
theme first appears like a delicate, hardly distinguish-
able dream, in unbroken *pp*, and is then lost in a
melting *ritardando*; thereafter, by means of a *crescendo*,
it enters its true sphere, and proceeds to unfold its
real nature. It is obviously the delicate duty of the
executants to indicate the character of the new
movement with an appropriate modification of
tempo—*i.e.*, to take the notes which immediately

succeed the Adagio  for a link,

and so unobtrusively to connect them with the

following  that a change in the

movement is hardly perceptible, and moreover so to
manage the *ritardando,* that the *crescendo,* which
comes after it, will introduce the master's quick tempo,
in such wise that the *molto vivace* now appears as the
rhythmical consequence of the increase of tone during
the crescendo.   But the modifications here indicated
are usually overlooked ; and the sense of artistic
propriety is outraged by a sudden and vulgar *vivace,*
as though the whole piece were meant for a jest, and
the gaiety had at last begun !   People seem to think
this " classical." *

I may have been too circumstantial, but the matter
is of incalculable importance.   Let us now proceed to
look still more closely into the wants and requirements of a proper performance of classical music.

* For further comments upon this Quartet see Appendix B.

IN the foregoing investigations I hoped to have elucidated the problem of the modification of tempo, and to have shewn how a discerning mind will recognise and solve the difficulties inherent in modern classical music. Beethoven has furnished the immortal type of what I may call emotional, sentimental music— it unites all the separate and peculiar constituents of the earlier essentially naïve types; sustained and interrupted tone, cantilena and figurations, are no longer kept formally asunder—the manifold changes of a series of variations are not merely strung together, but are now brought into immediate contact, and made to merge one into the other. Assuredly, the novel and infinitely various combinations of a symphonic movement must be set in motion in an adequate and appropriate manner if the whole is not to appear as a monstrosity. I remember in my young days to have heard older musicians make very dubious remarks about the *Eroïca*.* Dionys Weber, at Prague, simply treated it as a

* Beethoven's Symphony, No. III.

nonentity. The man was right in his way; he chose to recognise nothing but the Mozartian Allegro; and in the strict tempo peculiar to that Allegro, he taught his pupils at the Conservatorium to play the *Eroïca!* The result was such that one could not help agreeing with him. Yet everywhere else the work was thus played, and it is still so played to this day! True, the symphony is now received with universal acclamations; but, if we are not to laugh at the whole thing, the real reasons for its success must be sought in the fact that Beethoven's music is studied apart from the concert-rooms—particularly at the piano—and its irresistible power is thus fully felt, though in rather a round-about way. If fate had not furnished such a path of safety, and if our noblest music depended solely upon the conductors, it would have perished long ago.

To support so astounding an assertion I will take a popular example:—Has not every German heard the overture to *Der Freyschütz* over and over again? I have been told of sundry persons who were surprised to find how frequently they had listened to this wonderful musical poem, without having been shocked when it was rendered in the most trivial manner; these persons were among the audience of a concert given at Vienna in 1864, when I was invited to conduct the overture. At the rehearsal it came to pass that the orchestra of the imperial opera (certainly one of the finest orchestras in existence), were surprised at my demands regarding the execution of this piece.

It appeared at once that the Adagio of the introduction had habitually been taken as a pleasant Andante in the tempo of the "Alphorn,"* or some such comfortable composition. That this was not "Viennese tradition" only, but had come to be the universal practice, I had already learnt at Dresden — where Weber himself had conducted his work. When I had a chance to conduct Der Freyschütz at Dresden—eighteen years after Weber's death—I ventured to set aside the slovenly manner of execution which had prevailed under Reissiger, my senior colleague. I simply took the tempo of the introduction to the overture as I felt it; whereupon a veteran member of the orchestra, the old violoncellist Dotzauer, turned towards me and said seriously: "Yes, this is the way Weber himself took it; I now hear it again correctly for the first time." Weber's widow, who still resided at Dresden, became touchingly solicitous for my welfare in the position of Capellmeister. She trusted that my sympathy with her deceased husband's music would bring about correct performances of his works, for which she had no longer dared to hope. The recollection of this flattering testimony has frequently cheered and encouraged me. At Vienna I was bold enough to insist upon a proper performance. The orchestra actually *studied* the too-well-known overture anew. Discreetly led by R. Lewi, the Cornists

---

* A sentimental song by Proch.

entirely changed the tone of the soft woodnotes in the introduction, which they had been accustomed to play as a pompous show piece. The magic perfume of the melody for the horns was now shed over the *Pianissimo* indicated in the score for the strings. Once only (also as indicated) the power of their tone rose to a mezzoforte and was then gradually lost again without the customary *sforzando*, in the delicately

inflected

The Violoncellos similarly reduced the usual heavy

accent  , which was now

heard above the tremolo of the violins like the delicate sigh it is intended to be, and which finally gave to the fortissimo that follows the crescendo that air of desperation which properly belongs to it. Having restored the mysterious dignity of the introductory Adagio, I allowed the wild movement of the Allegro to run its passionate course, without regard to the quieter expression, which the soft second theme demands ; for I knew that I should be able *sufficiently to slacken the pace at the right moment*, so that the proper movement for this theme might be reached.

Evidently the greater number, if not all modern Allegro movements, consist of a combination of two

essentially different constituent parts : in contrast
with the older naïve unmixed Allegro, the construction
is enriched by the combination of the pure Allegro
with the thematic peculiarities of the vocal Adagio in
all its gradations. The second theme of the overture
to " Oberon,"

which does not in the least partake of the character
of the Allegro, very clearly shows this contrasted
peculiarity. Technically, the composer has managed
to merge the character of this theme into the general
character of the piece. That is to say : on the
surface, the theme reads smoothly, according to the
scheme of an Allegro ; but, as soon as the true
character of the theme is brought out, it becomes
apparent that *a composer must think such a scheme capable
of considerable modification if it is to combine both principles.*
(Hauptcharactere.)

To continue the account of the performance of the
Freyschütz overture at Vienna : after the extreme
excitement of the tempo Allegro, I made use of the
long drawn notes of the clarinet—the character of
which is quite that of the Adagio—

so as imperceptibly to ease the tempo in this place, where the figurated movement is dissolved into sustained or tremulous tone ; so that, in spite of the connecting figure :

which renews the movement, and so beautifully leads to the cantilena in E flat, we had arrived at the very slight *nuance* of the main tempo, which has been kept up all along. I arranged with the excellent executants that they were to play this theme

legato, and with an equable piano, *i.e.*, without the customary commonplace accentuation and *not* as follows :

The good result was at once apparent, so that for the gradual reanimation of the tempo with the pulsating

I had only to give the slightest indication of the pace to find the orchestra perfectly ready to attack the most energetic *nuance* of the main tempo together with the following fortissimo. It was not so easy on the return of the conflict of the two strongly contrasted motives, to bring them out clearly without disturbing the proper feeling for the predominant rate of speed. Here, when the despairing energy of the allegro is concentrated in successively shorter periods, and culminates in

the success of the ever-present modification of tempo was perhaps shown best of all.

After the splendidly sustained C major chords, and the significant long pauses, by which these chords are so well relieved, the musicians were greatly surprised when I asked them to play the second theme, which is now raised to a joyous chant, *not* as they had been accustomed, in the violently excited *nuance* of the first allegro theme, but in the milder modification of the main time.

This worrying and driving to death of the *principal*

theme at the close of a piece is a habit common to all our orchestras—very frequently indeed nothing is wanting but the sound of the great horse-whip to complete the resemblance to the effects at a circus. No doubt increase of speed at the close of an over- ture is frequently demanded by composers; it is a matter of course in those cases where the true Allegro theme, as it were, remains in possession of the field, and finally celebrates its apotheosis; of which Beethoven's great overture to " Leonora " is a celebrated example. In this latter case, however, the effect of the increased speed of the Allegro is frequently spoilt by the fact that the conductor, who does not know how to modify the main tempo to meet the various requirements of the thematic combinations (*e.g.*, at the proper moment to relax the rate of speed), has already permitted the main tempo to grow so quick as to exclude the possibility of any further increase—unless, indeed, the strings choose to risk an abnormal rush and run, such as I remember to have heard with astonishment, though not with satisfaction, from this very Viennese orchestra. The necessity for such an eccentric exertion arose in con- sequence of the main tempo having been hurried too much during the progress of the piece ; the final result was simply an exaggeration—and moreover, a risk to which no true work of art should be exposed— though, in a rough way, it may be able to bear it.

However, it is difficult to understand why the close of the Freyschütz overture should be thus hurried and worried by Germans, who are supposed to possess some delicacy of feeling. Perhaps the blunder will appear less inexplicable, if it is remembered that this second cantilena, which towards the close is treated as a chant of joy, was, already at its very first appearance, made to trot on at the pace of the principal Allegro : like a pretty captive girl tied to the tail of a hussar's charger—and it would seem a case of simple practical justice that she should eventually be raised to the charger's back when the wicked rider has fallen off—whereat, finally, the Capellmeister is delighted, and proceeds to apply the great whip.

An indescribably repulsive effect is produced by this trivial reading of a passage, by which the composer meant to convey, as it were, a maiden's tender and warm effusions of gratitude. * Truly, certain people who sit and listen again and again to a vulgar effect such as this, whenever and wherever the Freyschütz overture is performed, and approve of it, and talk of "the wonted excellence of our orchestral performances"—and otherwise indulge in queer notions of their own about music, like the venerable Herr *Lobe*, † whose jubilee we have recently celebrated—such people, I say, are in the right

---

* See the close of the Aria in E, known as "Softly sighing," in Der Freyschütz (No. 8).

† Author of a " Kompositionslehre," " Briefe eines Wohlbe-kannten," etc.

position to warn the public against " the absurdities of a mistaken idealism "—and " to point towards that which is artistically genuine, true and eternally valid, as an antidote to all sorts of half-true or half-mad doctrines and maxims. "*

As I have related, a number of Viennese amateurs who attended a performance of this poor maltreated overture, heard it rendered in a very different manner. The effect of that performance is still felt at Vienna. People asserted that they could hardly recognize the piece, and wanted to know what I had done to it. They could not conceive how the novel and surprising effect at the close had been produced, and scarcely credited my assertion that a moderate tempo was the sole cause. The musicians in the orchestra, however, might have divulged a little secret, namely this :—in the fourth bar of the powerful and brilliant entrata

I interpreted the sign >, which in the score might be mistaken for a timid and senseless accent, as a mark of *diminuendo* ——— assuredly in accordance with the composer's intentions—thus we reached a more moderate degree of force, and the opening bars of the theme

* (See Eduard Bernsdorf in *Signale für die musicalishe Welt*, No. 67, 1869),

were at once distinguished by a softer inflection, which, I now could easily permit to swell to fortissimo—thus the warm and tender motive, gorgeously supported by the full orchestra, appeared happy and glorified.

Our Capellmeisters are not particularly pleased at a success such as this.

Herr Dessof, however, whose business it was afterwards to conduct " Der Freyschütz," at the Viennese opera, thought it advisable to leave the members of the orchestra undisturbed in the possession of the new reading.   He announced this to them, with a smile, saying : " Well, gentlemen, let us take the overture à la Wagner."

Yes, Yes:—à la Wagner! I believe, there would be no harm in taking a good many other things, à la Wagner ! *

At all events this was an entire concession on the part of the Viennese Capellmeister ; whereas in a similar case, my former colleague, the late Reissiger, would only consent to meet me *half* way.   In the last movement of Beethoven's A major symphony, I discovered a *piano* which Reissiger had been pleased to

* " Wagnerisch "—there is a pun here: wagen = to dare ; erwägen = to weigh mentally: thus " *Wag*nerisch," may be taken as—in a daring well considered manner.

insert in the parts when he conducted the work. This
piano concerned the grand preparation for the close of
this final movement, when, after the powerful
reiterated chords on the dominant seventh A
(Breitkopf and Haertel's Score, page 86) the figure

is carried on *forte*, until with "sempre più forte," it
becomes still more violent. This did not suit
Reissiger; accordingly, at the bar quoted, he interpo-
lated a sudden *piano*, so that he might in time get a
perceptible crescendo. Of course, I erased this piano
and restored the energetic forte in its integrity. And
thus, I presume, I again committed an offence against
"Lobe and Bernsdorf's eternal laws of truth and
beauty," which Reissiger, in his day, was so careful
to obey.

After I had left Dresden, when this A major
symphony came to be performed again under Reissiger,
he did not feel at ease about that passage; so he
stopped the orchestra, and advised that it should be
taken *mezzo forte!*

On another occasion (not very long ago, at Munich),
I was present at a public performance of the overture
to "*Egmont*," which proved instructive—somewhat
after the manner of the customary performances of
the overture to "Der Freyschütz."

In the *Allegro* of the Egmont overture * the powerful and weighty *sostenuto* of the introduction :

is used in rhythmical diminution as the first half of the second theme, and is answered in the other half, by a soft and smooth countermotive.

The conductor, † in accordance with "classical" custom, permitted this concise and concentrated theme, a contrast of power and gentle self-content, to be swept away by the rush of the Allegro, like a sere and withered leaf; so that, whenever it caught the ear at all, a sort of dance pace was heard, in which, during the two opening bars the dancers stepped forward, and in the two following bars twirled about in "Laendler" ‡ fashion.

When *Bülow*, in the absence of the favourite senior conductor, was called upon to lead the music to

* Beethoven: op. 84.   † Franz Lachner.

‡ Laendler—an Austrian peasant's dance, in triple time, from which the waltz is derived.

Egmont at Munich, I induced him, amongst other things, to attend to the proper rendering of this passage. It proved at once strikingly effective— concise, laconic—as Beethoven meant it. The tempo, which up to that point had been kept up with passionate animation, was firmly arrested, and very slightly modified—just as much, and no more than was necessary to permit the orchestra properly to attack this thematic combination, so full of energetic decision and of a contemplative sense of happiness. At the end of the ¾ time the combination is treated in a broader and still more determined manner; and thus these simple, but indispensible, modifications brought about a new reading of the overture—the *correct* reading. The impression produced by this properly conducted performance was singular, to say the least of it; I was assured that the manager of the Court theatre was persuaded there had been "a break-down."

No one among the audience of the celebrated Odeon Concerts at Munich dreamt of "a break-down" when the above-mentioned senior "classical" conductor led the performance of Mozart's G minor symphony, when I happened to be present. The manner in which the *Andante* of the symphony was played, and the effect it produced was altogether surprising. Who has not, in his youth, admired this beautiful piece, and tried to realize it in his own way? In what way? No matter. If the marks of expression are scanty, the wonderful composition

arouses one's feelings; and fancy supplies the means
to read it in accordance with such feelings. It seems
as though Mozart had expected something of the
kind, for he has given but few and meagre indications
of the expression. So we felt free to indulge ourselves
in the delicately increasing swing of the quavers, with
the moon-like rise of the violins :

the notes of which we believed to sound softly legato;
the tenderly whispering

touched us as with wings of angels, and before the
solemn admonitions and questionings of

(which, however, we heard in a finely sustained
crescendo) we imagined ourselves led to a blissful
evanescence, which came upon us with the final bars.
Fancies of this sort, however, were not permitted
during the " strictly classical " performance, under

the veteran Capellmeister, at the Munich Odeon; the proceedings, there, were carried on with a degree of solemnity, enough to make one's flesh creep, with a sensation akin to a foretaste of eternal perdition.

The lightly floating Andante was converted into a ponderous *Largo;* not the hundredth part of the weight of a single quaver was spared us; stiff and ghastly, like a bronze pigtail, the *battuta* of this Andante was swung over our heads; even the feathers on the angel's wings were turned into corkscrew curls—rigid, like those of the seven year's war. Already, I felt myself placed under the staff of a Prussian recruiting officer, A.D. 1740, and longed to be bought off—but! who can guess my terror, when the veteran turned back the pages, and recommenced his Largo-Andante, merely to do " classical " justice to the two little dots before the double bar in the score! I looked about me for help and succour—and beheld another wondrous thing: the audience listened patiently: quite convinced that everything was in the best possible order, and that they were having a true Mozartian " feast for the ears " in all innocence and safety.—This being so, I acquiesced, and bowed my head in silence.

Once, however, a little later on, my patience failed. At a rehearsal of " Tannhäuser " I had quietly allowed a good deal to pass by unnoticed—even the clerical tempo at which my knights had to march up in the second act. But now it became evident that the undoubtedly " veteran " master could not even make

out how $\frac{4}{4}$ time was to be changed to an equivalent
$\frac{6}{4}$: *i.e.*, two crotchets

into a triplet of three crotchets

The trouble arose during Tannhäuser's narrative
of his pilgrimage (Act III.), when $\frac{4}{4}$

is replaced by $\frac{6}{4}$

This was too much for the veteran. He was very
properly accustomed to beat $\frac{4}{4}$ on the square; but it
is also the custom of such conductors to beat
$\frac{6}{4}$ after the manner of $\frac{6}{8}$, that is, with an *Alla breve*
beat—two in the bar. (Only in the Andante of the
G minor symphony did I witness six grave quaver
beats = 1, 2, 3,—4, 5, 6). But, for my poor narrative
about the Pope at Rome, the conductor thought two
timid *Alla breve* beats sufficient—so that the members
of the orchestra might be left at liberty to make out
the crotchets as best they could. Thus it came to
pass that the tempo was taken at exactly double the
proper pace: namely, instead of the equivalents just
described, things appeared thus :

Now, this may have been very interesting, musically, but it compelled the poor singer of Tannhäuser to relate his painful recollections of Rome to a gay and lively waltz-rhythm (which, again, reminds me of Lohengrin's narrative about the Holy Grail, at Wiesbaden, where I heard it recited *scherzando*, as though it were about Queen Mab). But as I was, in this case, dealing with so excellent a representative of Tannhäuser as *Ludwig Schnorr*,* I was bound to establish the right tempo, and, for once, respectfully to interfere. This, I am sorry to say, caused some scandal and annoyance. I fear in course of time, it even caused some little martyrdom, and inspired a cold-blooded Gospel-critic† to celebrate and console the veteran-martyr in a couple of sonnets. Indeed, we have now got sundry " martyrs of classical music " crowned with a halo of poetry. I shall beg leave to examine them still more closely in the sequel.

* Ludwig Schnorr von Carolsfeld, the first "Tristan" died 1865.

† David Strauss, author of " Das Leben Jesu."

IT has repeatedly been pointed out that our conductors dislike attempts at modification of tempo, for the sake of perspicuity in the rendering of Beethoven and other classical music. I have shewn that plausible objections can be urged against such modifications, so long as they are not accompanied by corresponding modifications of tone and expression; and I have further shewn that such objections have no foundation other than the incompetence of conductors, who attempt to perform functions for which they are not fit. In fact, there is but one valid objection which can be urged against the mode of procedure I advocate, namely this: nothing can be more detrimental to a piece of music than *arbitrary nuances* of tempo, etc., such as are likely to be introduced by this or that self-willed and conceited time-beater, for the sake of what he may deem " effective." In that way, certainly, the very existence of our classical music might, in course of time, be undermined. Now, what is to be said or done in the face of so sad a state of things ?

A sound public opinion with regard to questions of art does not exist in Germany ; and there is nothing amongst us that could effectually put a stop to such vagaries.   Thus, the above objection, valid as it is (though seldom put forward in good faith), again points towards the conductors ; for, if incompetent persons are not to be permitted to maltreat classical music at their pleasure, how is it that the best and most influential musicians have not taken this matter in hand? why have they themselves led classical music into such a groove of triviality and actual disfigurement ?   In many instances the objection in question is merely put forward as a pretext for opposition to all efforts in the direction I have indicated.   Indolent and incompetent persons form   an   immense   majority: and, under certain circumstances, incompetency and sluggishness unite, and grow aggressive.

The first performances of classical compositions with us have, as a rule, been very imperfect.   (One has but to recall the accounts of the circumstances under which Beethoven's   most   difficult   symphonies   were   first performed!).   A good deal also has, from the first, been brought before the German public in an absolutely incorrect   manner   (compare   my   essay   on   " Gluck's Overture to Iphigenia in Aulis " in one of the earlier volumes of the " Neue Zeitschrift für Musik.") *   This being so, how can the current style of execution appear other than it is ?   In Germany the " conservators "

* Wagner, " Gesammelte Schriften," Vol. V., p. 143.

of such works are both ignorant and incompetent.
And, on the other hand, suppose one were to take an
unprejudiced and impartial view of the manner in
which a master like *Mendelssohn* led such works!
How can it be expected that lesser musicians, not to
speak of musical mediocrities generally, should really
comprehend things which have remained doubtful to
their master? For average people, who are not
specially gifted, there is but one good guide to
excellence—a good example; and a guiding example
was not to be found in the path chosen by the host of
mediocrities. Unfortunately, they entirely occupy this
path or pass, at present,—without a guide or leader—
and any other person who might, perchance, be capable
of setting up a proper example, has no room left.
For these reasons I deem it worth while to strip this
spirit of reticence and shallow pretence of the halo of
sanctity with which it poses as the "chaste spirit of
German art." A poor and pretentious pietism at
present stifles every effort, and shuts out every breath
of fresh air from the musical atmosphere. At this rate
we may live to see our glorious music turned into a
colourless and ridiculous bug-bear!

I therefore think it advisable to take a straightforward survey of this spirit, to look closely into its
eyes, and to openly assert that it has *nothing* in
common with the true spirit of German music. It is
not easy to estimate the positive weight and value of
modern, Beethovenian, music—but we may perhaps
hope to get at some negative proof of its worth, by an

examination of the pseudo-Beethovenian-classicism now in the ascendant.

It is curious to note how the opposition to the things I advocate finds vent in the press, where uneducated scribblers clamour and create a disturbance, whilst in the profession proper, the utterances are far from noisy, though sufficiently bitter. ("You see he cannot express himself," a lady once said to me with a sly glance at one of these reticent musicians). As I have said at the outset this new musical Areopagus consists of two distinct species : Germans of the old type, who have managed to hold out in the South of Germany, but are now gradually disappearing; and the elegant Cosmopolites, who have arisen from the school of Mendelssohn in the North, and are now in the ascendant. Formerly the two species did not think much of each other; but latterly, in the face of certain disturbances which seem to threaten their flourishing business, they have united in mutual admiration ; so that in the South the Mendelssohnian school, with all that pertains to it, is now lauded and protected—whilst, in the North, the prototype of South-German sterility is welcomed* with sudden and profound respect—an honour which Lindpaintner of blessed memory † did not live to see. Thus to ensure their prosperity the two species are shaking

* Franz Lachner, and his Orchestral Suites.

† Peter Josef von Lindpaintner, 1791-1856, Capellmeister at Stuttgart.

hands. Perhaps at the outset such an alliance was rather repugnant to those of the old native type; but they got over the difficulty by the aid of that not particularly laudable propensity of Germans : namely, a timid feeling of jealousy which accompanies a sense of helplessness (*die mit der Unbeholfenheit verbundene Scheelsucht*). This propensity spoilt the temper of one of the most eminent German musicians of later times,* led him to repudiate his true nature, and to submit to the regulations of the elegant and alien second species. The opposition of the more subordinate musicians signifies nothing beyond this : " we cannot advance, we do not want others to advance, and we are annoyed to see them advance in spite of us." This is at least honest Philistinism; dishonest only under provocation.

In the newly-formed camp, however, things are not so simple. Most complicated maxims have there been evolved from the queer ramifications of personal, social, and even national interests. Without going into details, I will only touch one prominent point, that *here there is a good deal to conceal, a good deal to hide and suppress.* The members of the fraternity hardly think it desirable to show that they are "*musicians*" at all; and they have sufficient reason for this.

Our true German musician was originally a man difficult to associate with. In days gone by the social

---

* Robert Schumann.

position of musicians in Germany, as in France
and England, was far from good. Princes, and
aristocratical society generally, hardly recognised
the social status of musicians (Italians alone
excepted). Italians were everywhere preferred to
native Germans (witness the treatment Mozart met
with at the Imperial Court at Vienna). Musicians
remained peculiar half-wild, half-childish beings, and
were treated as such by their employers. The education, even of the most gifted, bore traces of the fact that
they had not really come under the influence of refined
and intelligent society—(think of Beethoven when he
came in contact with Goethe at Teplitz). It was taken
for granted that the mental organization of professional
musicians was such as to render them insusceptible
to the influence of culture. When *Marschner,** in
1848, found me striving to awaken the spirit of the
members of the Dresden orchestra, he seriously dis-
suaded me, saying he thought professional musicians
incapable of understanding what I meant. Certain
it is, as I have already said, that the higher and
highest professional posts were formerly occupied
by men who had gradually risen from the ranks, and in
a good journeyman-like sense this had brought about
many an excellent result. A certain family feeling, not
devoid of warmth and depth, was developed in such
patriarchal orchestras—and this family feeling was ready

---

* Heinrich Marschner, 1796-1861, operatic composer; Weber's
colleague at Dresden, subsequently conductor at Leipzig and
Hanover.

to respond to the suggestions of a sympathetic leader. But just as, for instance, the Jews formerly kept aloof from our handicraftsmen, so the new species of conductors did not grow up among the musical guilds—they would have shrunk from the hard work there. They simply took the lead of the guilds—much as the bankers take the lead in our industrial society. To be able to do this creditably conductors had to show themselves possessed of something that was lacking to the musicians from the ranks—something at least very difficult to acquire in a sufficient degree, if it was not altogether lacking: namely, a certain varnish of culture (Gebildetheit). As a banker is equipped with capital, so our elegant conductors are the possessors of pseudo-culture. I say pseudo-culture, not *culture*, for whoever really possesses the latter is a superior person and above ridicule. But there can be no harm in discussing our varnished and elegant friends.

I have not met with a case in which the results of true culture, an open mind and a free spirit, have become apparent amongst them. Even Mendelssohn, whose manifold gifts had been cultivated most assiduously, never got over a certain anxious timidity; and in spite of all his well-merited successes, he remained outside the pale of German art-life. It seems probable that a feeling of isolation and constraint was a source of much pain to him, and shortened his life. The reason for this is to be found in the fact that the motives of a desire for culture, such as his, lack spontaneity—(*dass dem Motive eines solchen*

Bildungsdranges keine Unbefangenheit innewohnt) — and
arise from a desire to cover and conceal some part
of a man's individuality, rather than to develop it
freely.

But true culture is not the result of such a
process : a man may grow extremely intelligent in
certain ways ; yet the point at which these ways meet
may be other than that of " pure intelligence " (*rein-
schende Intelligenz*).   To watch such an inner process in
the case of a particularly gifted and delicately organized
individual is sometimes touching ; in the case of lesser
and more trivial natures however, the contemplation
of the process and its results is simply nauseous.

Flat and empty pseudo-culture confronts us with a
grin, and if we are not inclined to grin in return, as
superficial observers of our civilization are wont to do,
we   may   indeed   grow   seriously   indignant.   And
German musicians now-a-days have good reason to be
indignant if this miserable sham culture presumes to
judge of the spirit and significance of our glorious
music.

Generally speaking, it is a characteristic *trait* of
pseudo-culture not to insist too much, not to enter
deeply into a subject or, as the phrase goes, not to
make much fuss about anything.   Thus, whatever is
high, great and deep, is treated as a matter of course, a
commonplace, naturally at everybody's beck and call ;
something that can be readily acquired, and, if need
be, imitated.   Again, that which is sublime, god-like,
demonic, must not be dwelt upon, simply because it

is impossible or difficult to copy. Pseudo-culture accordingly talks of "excrescencies," "exaggerations," and the like—and sets up a novel system of æsthetics, which professes to rest upon *Goethe*—since he, too, was averse to prodigious monstrosities, and was good enough to invent "artistic calm and beauty" in lieu thereof. "The guileless innocence of art" becomes an object of laudation ; and *Schiller*, who now and then was too violent, is treated rather contemptuously ; so, in sage accord with the Philistines of the day, a new conception of classicality is evolved. In other departments of art, too, the Greeks are pressed into service, on the ground that Greece was the very home of " clear transparent serenity ; " and, finally, such shallow meddling with all that is most earnest and terrible in the existence of man, is gathered together in a full and novel philosophical system *—wherein our varnished musical heroes find a comfortable and undisputed place of honour.

How the latter heroes treat great musical works I have shewn by the aid of a few representative examples. It remains to explain the serene and cheerful Greek sense of that "getting over the ground" which Mendelssohn so earnestly recommended. This will be best shown by a reference to his disciples and successors. Mendelssohn wished to hide the inevitable shortcomings of the execution, and also, in case of need, the shortcomings of that which is executed ;

* Hanslick's " Vom Musicalish-Schoenen," and particularly Vischer's voluminous " System der Æsthetik."

to this, his disciples and successors superadded the specific motive of their "*culture*": namely, "to hide and cover up in general," to escape attention, to create no disturbance. There is a *quasi* physiological reason for this which I accidentally discovered once upon a time.

For the performance of *Tannhäuser*, at Paris, I re-wrote the scene in the "Venusberg" on a larger scale: at one of the rehearsals I explained to the ballet master that the little tripping *pas* of his Mænads and Bacchantes contrasted miserably with my music, and asked him to arrange something wild and bold for his corps—something akin to the groups of Bacchantes on ancient bas-reliefs. Thereupon the man whistled through his fingers, and said, "Ah, I understand perfectly, but to produce anything of the sort I should require a host of *premiers sujets ;* if I were to whisper a word of what you say, and indicate the attitudes you intend to my people here, we should instantly have the 'cancan,' and be lost." The very same feeling which induced my Parisian ballet-master to rest content with the most vapid *pas* of Mænads and Bacchantes, forbids our elegant, new-fangled conductors to cut the traces of their "culture." They are afraid such a thing might lead to a scandal *à la* Offenbach. Meyerbeer was a warning to them ; the Parisian opera had tempted him into certain ambiguous semitic accentuations in music, which fairly scared the "men of culture."

A large part of their education has ever since consisted in learning to watch their behaviour, and to suppress any indications of passion; much as one who naturally lisps and stammers, is careful to keep quiet, lest he should be overcome by a fit of hissing and stuttering. Such continuous watchfulness has assisted in the removal of much that was unpleasant, and the general humane amalgamation has gone on much more smoothly; which, again, has brought it about that many a stiff and poorly developed element of our home-growth has been refreshed and rejuvenated. I have already mentioned that amongst musicians roughness of speech and behaviour are going out, that delicate details in musical execution are more carefully attended to, etc. But it is a very different thing to allow the necessity for reticence, and for the suppression of certain personal characteristics, to be converted into a principle for the treatment of our art! Germans are stiff and awkward when they want to appear mannerly : *but they are noble and superior when they grow warm.* And are we to suppress our fire to please those reticent persons? In truth, it looks as though they expected us to do so.

In former days, whenever I met a young musician who had come in contact with Mendelssohn, I learnt that the master had admonished him not to think of effect when composing, and to avoid everything that might prove meretriciously impressive. Now, this was very pleasant and soothing advice; and those pupils who adopted it, and remained true to the master, have indeed produced neither " impression nor meretricious effect ; " only, the advice seemed to me rather too negative, and I failed to see the value of that which was positively acquired under it. I believe the entire teaching of the Leipzig Conservatorium was based upon some such negative advice, and I understand that young people there have been positively pestered with warnings of a like kind ; whilst their best endeavours met with no encouragement from the masters, unless their taste in music fully coincided with the tone of the orthodox psalms. The first result of the new doctrine, and the most important for our investigations, came to light in the execution of classical music. Everything here was governed by the fear of exaggeration (*etwa in das Drastische zu fallen*). I have, for instance, hitherto not found any traces that those later pianoforte works of Beethoven, in which the master's peculiar style is best developed, have actually been studied and played by the converts to that doctrine.

For a long time I earnestly wished to meet with some one who could play the great Sonata in B flat (Op. 106) as it should be played. At length my wish was gratified—but by a person who came from a camp wherein those doctrines do *not* prevail. *Franz Liszt*, also, gratified my longing to hear *Bach*. No doubt Bach has been assiduously cultivated by Liszt's opponents; they esteem Bach for teaching purposes, since a smooth and mild manner of execution apparently accords better with his music than " modern effect," or Beethovenian strenuousness (*Drastik*).

I once asked one of the best-reputed older musicians,

a friend and companion of Mendelssohn (whom I
have already mentioned à propos of the tempo di menuetto
of the eighth symphony *), to play the eighth Prelude
and Fugue from the first part of " Das Wohltemperirte
Clavier " (E flat minor), a piece which has always had
a magical attraction for me.* He very kindly complied,
and I must confess that I have rarely been so
much taken by surprise. Certainly, there was no
trace here of sombre German gothicism and all
that old-fashioned stuff ; under the hands of my friend,
the piece ran along the keyboard with a degree of
" Greek serenity " that left me at a loss whither to
turn ; in my innocence I deemed myself transported to
a neo-hellenic synagogue, from the musical cultus of
which all old testamentary accentuations had been
most elegantly eliminated. This singular performance
still tingled in my ears, when at length I begged Liszt
for once to cleanse my musical soul of the painful
impression ; he played the fourth Prelude and Fugue
(C sharp minor). Now, I knew what to expect from
Liszt at the piano ; but I had not expected anything
like what I came to hear from Bach, though I had
studied him well; I saw how study is eclipsed by
genius. By his rendering of this single fugue of Bach's,
Liszt revealed Bach to me ; so that I henceforth knew
for certain what to make of Bach, and how to solve
all doubts concerning him. I was convinced, also,

* Ferdinand Hiller.

* i.e. Prelude VIII., from Part I. of Bach's 48 Preludes and
Fugues.

that *those* people know *nothing* of Bach ; and if anyone
chooses to doubt my assertion, I answer : "request
them to play a piece of Bach's." *

I would like further to question any member of that
musical temperance society and, if it has ever been his
lot to hear Liszt play Beethoven's great B flat Sonata,
I would ask him to testify honestly whether he had before
really known and understood that sonata ? I, at least, am
acquainted with a person who was so fortunate ; and
who was constrained to confess that he had not before
understood it. And to this day, who plays Bach,
and the great works of Beethoven, in public, and
compels every audience to confess as much ? a
member of that " school for temperance ?"   No ! it
is Liszt's chosen successor, *Hans von Bülow*.

So much for the present on this subject. It might
prove interesting to observe the attitude these reticent
gentlemen take up with regard to performances such as
Liszt's and Bülow's.

The successes of their policy, to which they are
indebted for the control of public music in Germany,
need not detain us ; but we are concerned in an
examination of the curious religious development within
their congregation. In this respect the earlier maxim,
" beware of effect "—the result of embarrassment
and cautious timidity—has now been changed, from a
delicate rule of prudence and security, to a positively
aggressive dogma. The adherents of this dogma
hypocritically look askance if they happen to meet

* See Appendix C,

with a true man in music. They pretend to be shocked, as though they had come across something improper. The spirit of their shyness, which originally served to conceal their own impotence, now attempts the defamation of other people's potency. Defamatory insinuations and calumny find ready acceptance with the representatives of German Philistinism, and appear to be at home in that mean and paltry state of things which, as we have seen, environs our musical affairs.

The principal ingredient, however, is an apparently judicious caution in presence of that which one happens to be incapable of, together with detraction of that which one would like to accomplish one's self. It is sad, above all things, to find a man so powerful and capable as *Robert Schumann* concerned in this confusion, and in the end to see his name inscribed on the banner of the new fraternity. The misfortune was that Schumann in his later days attempted certain tasks for which he was not qualified. And it is a pity to see that portion of his work, in which he failed to reach the mark he had set himself, raised as the insignia of the latest guild of musicians. A good deal of Schumann's early endeavour was most worthy of admiration and sympathy, and it has been cherished and nurtured by us (I am proud here to rank myself with Liszt's friends) in a more commendable and commending way than by his immediate adherents.* The latter, well aware that Schumann had herein evinced true productivity, knowingly kept

* See Appendix D.

these things in the background, perhaps because they could not play them in an effective way. On the other hand, certain works of Schumann conceived on a larger and bolder scale, and in which the limits of his gifts become apparent are now carefully brought forward.* The public does not exactly like these works, but their performance offers an opportunity to point out how commendable a thing it is to "make no effect." Finally, a comparison with the works of Beethoven in his third period (played as they play them) comes in opportunely.

Certain later, inflated (*schwülstig*) and dull productions of R. Schumann, which simply require to be played smoothly (*glatt herunter gespielt*) are confounded with Beethoven; and an attempt is made to shew that they agree in spirit with the rarest, boldest and most profound achievements of German music! Thus Schumann's shallow bombast is made to pass for the equivalent of the inexpressible purport of Beethoven—but always with the reservation that strenuous eccentricity such as Beethoven's is hardly admissible; whereas, vapid emptiness (*das gleichgiltig Nichtssagende*) is right and proper: a point at which Schumann properly played, and Beethoven improperly rendered, are perhaps comparable without much fear of misunderstanding! Thus these singular defenders of musical chastity stand towards our great classical

---

* Such as the Overtures to Faust, Die Braut von Messina, Julius Cæsar; the "Balladen," Das Glück von Edenhall, Des Sänger Fluch, Vom Pagen und der Königstochter, etc.

music in the position of eunuchs in the Grand-Turk's Harem ; and by the same token German Philistinism is ready to entrust them with the care of music in the family—since it is plain that anything ambiguous is not likely to proceed from that quarter.

But now what becomes of our great and glorious German music ? It is the fate of our music that really concerns us. We have little reason to grieve if, after a century of wondrous productivity, nothing particular happens to come to light for some little time. But there is every reason to beware of suspicious persons who set themselves up as the trustees and conservators of the "true German spirit" of our inheritance.

Regarded as individuals, there is not much to blame in these musicians; most of them compose very well. Herr Johannes Brahms once had the kindness to play a composition of his own to me—a piece with very serious variations—which I thought excellent, and from which I gathered that he was impervious to a joke. His performance of other pianoforte music at a concert gave me less pleasure. I even thought it impertinent that the friends of this gentleman pro-fessed themselves unable to attribute anything beyond "extraordinary technical power" to "Liszt and his school," whilst the execution of Herr Brahms appeared so painfully dry, inflexible and wooden. I should have liked to see Herr Brahms' technique annointed with a little of the oil of Liszt's school; an ointment which does not seem to issue spontaneously from the keyboard, but is evidently got

from a more aetherial region than that of mere
" technique." To all appearances, however, this was
a very respectable phenomenon ; only it remains
doubtful how such a phenomenon could be set up in
a natural way as the Messiah, or, at least, the
Messiah's most beloved disciple ; unless, indeed, an
affected enthusiasm for mediæval wood-carvings should
have induced us to accept those stiff wooden figures
for the ideals of ecclesiastical sanctity. In any case
we must protest against any presentation of our great
warm-hearted Beethoven in the guise of such sanctity.
If *they* cannot bring out the difference between Beethoven, whom they do not comprehend and therefore
pervert, and Schumann, who, for very simple reasons,
is incomprehensible, they shall, at least, not be permitted to assume that no difference exists.

I have already indicated sundry special aspects of
this sanctimoniousness. Following its aspirations a
little further we shall come upon a new field, across
which our investigation on and about conducting
must now lead us.

Some time ago the editor of a South German journal
discovered "hypocritical tendencies" (*muckerische Ten-
denzen*) in my artistic theories. The man evidently did
not know what he was saying; he merely wished to use
an unpleasant word. But my experience has led me
to understand that the essence of hypocrisy, and the
singular tendency of a repulsive sect of hypocrites
(Mucker), may be known by certain characteristics :—
they wish to be tempted, and greedily seek temptation,
in order to exercise their power of resistance !—Actual
scandal, however, does not begin until the secret of the
adepts and leaders of the sect is disclosed ;—the
adepts reverse the object of the resistance—they
resist with a view to increasing the ultimate sense of
beatitude. Accordingly, if this were applied to art, one
would perhaps not be saying a senseless thing if one
were to attribute hypocritical tendencies to the queer
"school for chastity" of this Musical Temperance
Society. The lower grades of the school may be conceived as vacillating between the orgiastic spirit of musical art and the reticence which their dogmatic maxim
imposes upon them—whilst it can easily be shewn that

the higher grades nourish a deep desire to enjoy that which is forbidden to the lower. The "Liebeslieder-Walzer" of the blessed Johannes (in spite of the silly title) might be taken as the exercises of the lower grades; whereas the intense longing after "the Opera," which troubles the sanctimonious devotions of the adepts, may be accepted as the mark of the higher and highest grades. If a single member, for once only, were to achieve a success with an opera, it is more than probable that the entire "school" would explode. But, somehow, no such success has hitherto been achieved, and this keeps the school together; for, every attempt that happens to fail, can be made to appear as a conscious effort of abstinence, in the sense of the exercises of the lower grades;* and "the opera," which beckons in the distance like a forlorn bride, can be made to figure as a symbol of the temptation, which is to be finally resisted—so that the authors of operatic failures may be glorified as special saints.

Seriously speaking, how do, these musical gentlemen stand with regard to "*the Opera?*" Having paid them a visit in the concert-room to which they belong, and from which they started, we shall now, for the sake of "conducting," look after them at the theatre.

Herr *Eduard Devrient,* in his "Erinnerungen," has given us an account of the difficulties his friend Mendelssohn met with in the search for a textbook to

---

* For a curious example of such exercises, see Ferdinand Hiller's "*Oper ohne Text*;" a set of pianoforte pieces, *à quatre mains.*

an opera. It was to be a truly "*German*" opera, and the master's friends were to find the materials wherewith to construct it. Unfortunately, they did not succeed in the quest. I suspect there were very simple reasons for this. A good deal can be got at by means of discussion and arrangement; but a "German" and "nobly-serene" opera, such as Mendelssohn in his delicate ambition dreamt of, is not exactly a thing that can be manufactured—nor old nor new testamentary recipes will serve the purpose. The master did not live to reach the goal: but his companions and apprentices continued their efforts. Herr Hiller believed he could force on a success, simply by dint of cheerful and unflagging perseverance. Everything, he thought, depends upon a "lucky hit," such as others had made in his very presence, and which steady perseverance, as in a game of chance, must, sooner or later, bring round to him. But the "lucky hit" invariably missed. Schumann also did not succeed,* and many other members of the church of abstinence, both adepts and neophytes, have since stretched forth their "chaste and innocent" hands in search of an operatic success—they troubled greatly— but their efforts proved fruitless—"the fortunate grip" failed.

Now, such experiences are apt to embitter the most harmless persons. All the more so, since Capellmeisters and Musikdirectors are daily occupied at the

---

*Genoveva, "Oper in vier Acten, nach Tieck und F. Hebbel, Musik von Robert Schumann. Op. 81."

theatres, and are bound to serve in a sphere in which they are absolutely helpless and impotent. And the causes of their impotence, with regard to the composition of an opera, are also the causes of their inability to conduct an opera properly. Yet such is the fate of our public art, that gentlemen who are not even able to conduct concert music, are the sole leaders in the very complicated business of the opera theatres! Let a reader of discretion imagine the condition of things there!

I have been prolix in showing the weakness of our conductors, in the very field, where, by rights, they ought to feel at home. I can be brief now with regard to the opera. Here it simply comes to this: " Father, forgive them; for they know not what they do." To characterize their disgraceful doings, I should have to show how much that is good and significant *might* be done at the theatres, and this would lead me too far. Let it be reserved for another occasion. For the present I shall only say a little about their ways as operatic conductors.

In the concert room these gentlemen go to work with the most serious mien; at the opera they deem it becoming to put on a nonchalant, sceptical, cleverly-frivolous air. They concede with a smile that they are not quite at home in the opera, and do not profess to understand much about things which they do not particularly esteem. Accordingly, they are very accommodating and complaisant towards vocalists, female and male, for whom they are glad to make matters comfortable; they arrange the *tempo*, introduce fermatas, ritardandos, accelerandos, transpositions, and, above all, "cuts," whenever and wherever a vocalist chooses to call for such. Whence indeed are they to derive the authority to resist this or that absurd demand? If, perchance, a pedantically disposed conductor should incline to insist upon this or that detail, he will, as a rule, be found in the wrong. For vocalists are at least at home and, in their own frivolous way, at ease in the opera; they know well enough what they can do, and how to do it; so that, if anything worthy of admiration is produced in the operatic world it is generally due to the right instincts of the vocalists, just as in the orchestra the merit lies almost entirely in the good sense of the musicians. One has only to examine an orchestra part of " Norma," for instance, to see what a curious musical changeling (*Wechselbalg*) such innocent looking sheets of music paper can be turned into; the mere succession of the transpositions—the Adagio of an Aria in F sharp major, the Allegro in F, and between the two (for the sake of the military band) a transition in E flat—offers a truly horrifying picture of the music to which such an esteemed conductor cheerfully beats time.

It was only at a suburban theatre at Turin (*i.e.*, in Italy) that I witnessed a correct and complete performance of the " Barber of Seville;" for our conductors grudge the trouble it takes to do justice even to a simple score such as " Il Barbiere." They have no notion that a perfectly correct perform-

ance, be it of the most insignificant opera can produce
an excellent impression upon an educated mind, simply
by reason of its correctness.   Even the shallowest
theatrical   concoctions,   at   the   smallest   Parisian
theatres, can produce a pleasant æsthetical effect,
since, as a rule, they are carefully rehearsed, and
correctly rendered.   The power of the artistic principle
is, in fact, so great that an æsthetic result is at once
attained, if only some part of that principle be properly
applied, and its conditions fulfilled : and such is true
art, although it may be on a very low level.   But we
do not get such æsthetic results in Germany, unless
it be at *performances of Ballets*, in Vienna, or Berlin.
Here the whole matter is in the hands of one man—
the ballet-master—and that man knows his business.
Fortunately, he is in a position to dictate the rate of
movement to the orchestra, for the expression as well
as for the *tempo*, and he does so, not according to his
individual whim, like an operatic singer, but with a
view to the *ensemble*, the consensus of all the artistic
factors; and now, of a sudden, it comes to pass that
the orchestra plays correctly !   A rare sense of satisfaction will be felt by everyone who, after the tortures of
an opera, witnesses a performance of one of those
Ballets.

In this way the stage manager might lend his aid to
the *ensemble* of the opera.   But, singularly enough,
the fiction that the opera is a branch of absolute music
is everywhere kept up ; every vocalist is aware of the
musical director's ignorance of the business of an

opera ; yet—if it should happen that the right instincts
of gifted singers, musicians and executants generally
are aroused by a fine work, and bring about a successful performance—are we not accustomed to see the Herr
Capellmeister called to the front, and otherwise
rewarded, as the representative of the total artistic
achievement ?   Ought he not himself to be surprised
at this ?   Is he not, in his turn, in a position to pray,
" Forgive them, they know not what they do ?"

But as I wished to speak of Conducting proper,
and do not want to lose my way in the operatic
wilderness, I have only to confess that I have come
to the end of this chapter.   I cannot dispute about
the conducting of our capellmeisters at the theatres.
Singers may do so, when they have to complain that
this conductor is not accommodating enough, or that
the other one does not give them their cues properly :
in short, from the stand-point of vulgar journeyman-
work, a discussion may be possible.   *But from the point
of view of truly artistic work this sort of conducting cannot be
taken into account at all.*   Among Germans, now living,
I am, perhaps, the only person who can venture openly
to pronounce so general a condemnation, and I
maintain that I am not exceeding the limits of my
province when I do so.

If I try to sum up my experiences, regarding performances of my own operas, I am at a loss to distinguish
with which of the qualities of our conductors I am
concerned.   Is it the spirit in which they treat
German music in the concert rooms, or the spirit

in which they deal with the opera at the theatres?
I believe it to be my particular and personal misfortune
that the two spirits meet in my operas, and mutually
encourage one another in a rather dubious kind
of way. Whenever the former spirit, which
practices upon our classical concert music, gets a
chance—as in the instrumental introductions to my
operas—I have invariably discovered the disastrous
consequences of the bad habits already described at
such length. I need only speak of the *tempo*, which
is either absurdly hurried (as, for instance, under
Mendelssohn, who, once upon a time, at a Leipzig
Gewandhaus concert, produced the overture to
Tannhäuser as an example and a warning), or muddled
(like the introduction to Lohengrin at Berlin, and
almost everywhere else), or both dragged and muddled
(like the introduction to " Die Meistersinger," lately,
at Dresden and at other places), yet never with those
well-considered modifications of the *tempo*, upon
which I must count as much as upon the correct
intonation of the notes themselves, if an intelligible
rendering is to be obtained.

To convey some notion of faulty performances of
the latter sort it will suffice to point to the way in
which the overture to " Die Meistersinger " is usually
given. The main *tempo* of this piece is indicated
as " *sehr mässig bewegt* " (with very moderate movement);
according to the older method, it would have been
marked *Allegro maestoso*. Now, when this kind
of *tempo* continues through a long piece, particularly

if the themes are treated episodically, it demands
modification as much as, or even more than any
other kind of *tempo*; it is frequently chosen to embody
the manifold combinations of distinct motives; and
its broad divisions into regular bars of four beats
are found convenient, as these tend to render modifications of movement both easy and simple. This
moderate $\frac{4}{4}$ time can be interpreted in many and
various ways; it may consist of four vigorous crotchet-
beats, and thus express a true animated Allegro
(this is the main *tempo* I intend, which becomes most
animated in those eight bars of transition

which lead from the march proper to the theme in
E major); or, it may be taken to consist of a demi-
period made up of two $\frac{2}{4}$ beats; as when, at the
entrance of the shortened theme,

it assumes the character of a lively *Scherzando*; or,
it may even be interpreted as *Alla breve* ($\frac{2}{2}$ time)
when it would represent the older, easily moving
Tempo andante (often employed in church music) which

is to be rendered with two moderately slow beats to a bar. I have used it in the latter sense, beginning from the eighth bar after the return to C major, in a combination of the principal march theme, now allotted to the basses, with the second main theme, now sung broadly and with commodious ease, in rhythmical prolongation, by the violins and violon-cellos:

This second theme has previously been introduced in diminution, and in common $\frac{4}{4}$ time :

Together with the greatest delicacy which the proper execution demands, it here exhibits a passionate, almost hasty character (something like a whispered declaration of love). Not to disturb the main characteristic, delicacy, it is, therefore, necessary slightly to hold back the *tempo* (the moving figuration sufficiently expresses passionate haste), thus the extreme *nuance* of the main *tempo*, in the direction of a somewhat grave $\frac{4}{4}$ time, should be adopted here, and, to do this without a wrench (*i.e.*, without really

disfiguring the general character of the main *tempo*),
a bar is marked *poco rallentando*, to introduce the
change. Through the more restless *nuance* of this
theme :

which, eventually, gets the upper hand, and which is
indicated with " *leidenschaftlicher* " (more passionate)
it is easy to lead the *tempo* back into the original
quicker movement, in which, finally, it will be found
capable to serve in the above-mentioned sense of
an *Andante alla breve*, whereby it is only needful to
recur to a *nuance* of the main *tempo*, which has
already been developed in the exposition of the
piece ; namely, I have allowed the final development of the pompous march theme to expand to a
lengthy coda of a cantabile character conceived in that
tempo *Andante alla breve*. As this full-toned cantabile

is preceded by the weighty crochets of the fanfare

the modification of the tempo must obviously begin at
the end of the crochets, that is to say with the more
sustained notes of the chord on the dominant which
introduces the cantabile. And, as this broader movement in minims continues for some time with an
increase in power and modulation, I thought conductors could be trusted to attain the proper increase
of speed; the more so, as such passages, when simply
left to the natural impulse of the executants always
induce a more animated *tempo*. Being myself an ex-
perienced conductor, I counted upon this as a matter
of course, and merely indicated the passage at which
the *tempo* returns to the original ¾ time, which any
musician will feel, at the return of the crochets and
in the changes of harmony.

At the conclusion of the overture the broader ¾ time,
quoted above in the powerfully sustained march-like
fanfare, returns again; the quick figured embellish-
ments are added, and the *tempo* ends exactly as it
began.

This overture was first performed at a concert
at Leipzig, when I conducted it as described above.
It was so well played by the orchestra that the small
audience, consisting for the most part of non-resident
friends, demanded an immediate repetition, which the
musicians, who agreed with the audience, gladly
accorded. The favourable impression thus created

was much talked of, and the directors of the Gewandhaus Concerts decided to give the native Leipzig public a chance to hear the new overture.

In this instance Herr Capellmeister *Reinecke*, who had heard the piece under my direction, conducted it, and the very same orchestra played it—in such wise that the audience hissed ! I do not care to investigate how far this result was due to the straightforward honesty of the persons concerned ; let it suffice that competent musicians, who were present at the performance, described to me the *sort of time* the Herr Capellmeister had thought fit to beat to the overture— and therewith I knew enough.

If any conductor wishes to prove to his audience or to his directors, etc., what an ambiguous risk they will run with " Die Meistersinger," he need take no further trouble than to beat time to the overture after the fashion in which he is wont to beat it to the works of Beethoven, Mozart, and Bach (which fashion suits the works of R. Schumann fairly well); it will then be suffi-ciently obvious that he is dealing with a very unpleasant kind of music—let anyone imagine so animated, yet so sensitive a thing as the *tempo* which governs this overture, let this delicately constituted thing suddenly be forced into the Procrustus-bed of such a classical time-beater, what will become of it ? The doom is : " Herein shalt thou lie, whatsoever is too long with thee shall be chopped off, and whatsoever is too short shall be stretched ! " Whereupon the band strikes up and overpowers the cries of the victim !

Safely bedded in this wise, not only the overture, but, as will appear in the sequel, the entire opera of Die Meistersinger, or as much of it as was left after the Capellmeister's cuts, was presented to the public of Dresden. On this occasion, correctly and technically speaking, the merits of the conductor * consisted in this: he made a guess at the main *tempo*, chose the broadest *nuance* of it, and spread this over the whole, beating the steadiest and stiffest square time from beginning to end! The ultimate results were as follows: I had made use of the combination of the two main themes under an ideal *Tempo Andante alla breve* (quoted above from the conclusion of the overture, page 94) to form a pleasant and cheerful conclusion to the entire opera, something after the manner of a burden to some old popular song: I had augmented and enlarged the treatment of the thematic combination for this purpose, and now employed it as a sort of accompaniment to Hans Sachs's epilogising praise of the "Master-singers," and to his consolatory rhymes upon German art, with which the work ends. Though the words are serious, the closing apostrophe is none the less meant to have a cheering and hopeful effect; and, to produce this, I counted upon that simple thematic combination, the rhythmical movement of which was intended to proceed smoothly, and was not meant to assume a pompous character, except just before the end, when the chorus enters. Now in the overture, the conductor

---

* The late Julius Rietz.

had failed to see the necessity of a modification of the original march-like tempo in the direction of an *Andante alla breve*; and, of course, here—at the close of the opera—he equally failed to feel that the movement was not directly connected with the march *tempo*—his first mistake was therefore continued, and he proceeded to confine and hold fast the warmly-feeling singer of the part of Hans Sachs in rigid ¾ time, and to compel him to deliver his final address in the stiffest and most awkward manner possible. Friends of mine requested me to permit a large "cut" for Dresden, as the effect of the close was so very depressing. I declined ; and the complaints soon ceased. At length I came to understand the reason why ; the Capellmeister had acted for the obstinate composer ; "solely with a view to the good of the work," he had followed the dictates of his artistic insight and conscience, had laid his hands on the troublesome apostrophe, and simply "*cut*" it.

"Cut ! Cut !"—this is the *ultimo ratio* of our conductors ; by its aid they establish a satisfactory equilibrium between their own incompetence, and the proper execution of the artistic tasks before them. They remember the proverb : "What I know not, burns me not !" ("*was ich nicht weiss, macht mich nicht heiss*") and the public cannot object to an arrangement so eminently practical. It only remains for me to consider what I am to say to a performance of my work, which thus appears enclosed between a failure at Alpha, and a failure at Omega ?

Outwardly things look very pleasant: An unusually animated audience, and an ovation for the Herr Capell-meister—to join in which the royal father of my country returns to the front of his box. But, subsequently, ominous reports about cuts which had been made, and further changes and abbreviations super-added; whilst the impression of a perfectly unabbreviated, but perfectly correct performance, at Munich, remains in my mind, and makes it impossible for me to agree with the mutilators. So disgraceful a state of things seems inevitable, since few people understand the gravity of the evil, and fewer still care to assist in any attempts to mend it.

On the other hand there is some little consolation in the fact that in spite of all ill-treatment the work retains some of its power—that fatal power and "effect" against which the professors of the Leipsic conservatorium so earnestly warn their pupils, and against which all sorts of destructive tactics are applied in vain! Having made up my mind, not to assist personally at any future performance like the recent ones of "Die Meistersinger" at Dresden, I am content to accept the "success" of the work as a consolatory example illustrating the fate of our classical music in the hands of our conducting musicians. Classical music retains its warmth, and continues to exist in spite of the maltreatment they subject it to. It appears truly indestructible: and the Spirit of German art may accept this indestructibility as a consoling fact, and may fearlessly continue its efforts in future.

It might be asked : But what do the queer conductors with celebrated names amount to, considered simply as practical musicians? Looking at their perfect unanimity in every practical matter one might be led to think that, after all, they understand their business properly, and that, in spite of the protest of one's feelings, their ways might even be "classical." The general public is so ready to take the excellence of their doings for granted, and to accept it as a matter of course, that the middle-class musical people are not troubled with the slightest doubt as to who is to beat time at their musical festivals, or on any other great occasion when the nation desires to hear some music. No one but Herr Hiller, Herr Rietz, or Herr Lachner is thought fit for this. It would be simply impossible to celebrate the hundredth anniversary of Beethoven's birth if these three gentlemen should happen suddenly to sprain their wrists. On the other hand, I am sorry to say I know of no one to whom I would confidently entrust a single tempo in one of my operas ; certainly to no member of the staff of our army of time-beaters. Now and then I have met with some poor devil who showed real skill and talent for conduct-ing : but such rare fellows find it difficult to get on, because they are apt not only to see through the in-competence of the celebrities, but imprudent enough to speak about it. If, for instance, a man happens to discover serious mistakes in the orchestra parts of "Figaro," from which the opera had been played with special unction—heaven knows how often—under the solemn conductorship of a celebrity, he is not likely to gain the favour of his chief. Such gifted poor fellows are destined to perish like the heretics of old.

As everything is thus apparently in good order, and seems likely to remain so, I am again tempted to ask how *can* this be? We entertain lurking doubts whether these gentlemen really *are* musicians; evidently they do not evince the slightest *musical feeling*; yet, in fact, they *hear* very accurately (with mathematical, not ideal, accuracy; *contretemps* like that of the faulty orchestra parts do not happen to everyone); they are quick at a score, read and play at sight (many of them, at least, do so); in short, they prove true professionals; but, alongside of this, their general education (Bildung)— in spite of all efforts—is such as can pass muster in the case of a musician only; so that, if music were struck from the list of their attainments, there would be little left—least of all, a man of spirit and sense. No, no! they certainly *are* musicians and very competent musicians, who know and can do everything that pertains to music. Well, then? As soon as they begin to perform music they muddle matters, and feel unsafe all round, unless it be in " Ewig, selig," or at best in " Lord Sabaoth!"

That which makes our great music great is the very thing which confuses these people; unfortunately, this cannot be expressed in words and concepts, nor in arithmetical figures. Yet, what is it other than music? and music only! What, then, can be the reason of this barrenness, dryness, coldness, this complete inability to feel the influence of true music, and, in its presence, to forget any little vexation, any small jealous distress, or any mistaken personal notion ?   Could Mozart's astonishing gift for arithmetic serve us for a vague explanation? On the one hand, it seems that with him—whose nervous system was so excessively sensitive to any disturbing sound, whose heart beat with such overflowing sympathy—the ideal elements of music met and united to form a wondrous whole.   On the other hand, *Beethoven's* naïve way of adding up his accounts is sufficiently well known ; arithmetical problems of any sort or kind assuredly never entered into his social or musical plans.   Compared with Mozart he appears as a *monstrum per excessum* in the direction of sensibility, which, not being checked and balanced by an intellectual counterweight from the arithmetical side, can hardly be conceived as able to exist or to escape premature destruction, if it had not fortunately been protected by a singularly tough and robust constitution.   Nor can anything in Beethoven's music be gauged or measured by figures ; whilst with Mozart a good deal that appears regular—almost too regular (as has already been touched upon) is conceivable, and can be explained as the result of a naïve mixture of those two extremes of musical perception.   Accordingly the professional musicians under examination appear as monstrosities in the direction of musical arithmetic ; and it is not difficult to understand how such musicians, endowed with the very reverse of a Beethovenian temperament, should succeed and flourish with a nervous system of the commonest kind.

If then our celebrated and uncelebrated conductors happen to be born for music only under the sign of Numbers (im Zeichen der Zahl), it would seem very desirable that some new school might be able to teach them the proper *tempo* for our music by the rule of three. I doubt whether they will ever acquire it in the simple way of musical feeling; wherefore, I believe, I have now reached the end of my task.

Perhaps the new school is already in sight. I understand that a " High-School of Music " has been established at Berlin, under the auspices of the Royal Academy of Arts and Sciences, and that the director-ship of the school has been entrusted to the celebrated violinist, Herr *Joachim.* To start such a school without Herr Joachim, if his services are available, would be a great mistake. I am inclined to hope for much from him; because everything I know and have heard concerning his method of playing proves that this virtuoso is a complete master of the style of execution I demand for our classical music. By the side of Liszt and his disciples he is the only living musician to whom I can point as a practical proof and example in support of the foregoing assertions. It is imma-terial whether or not Herr Joachim likes to see his name mentioned in such connection; for, with regard to that which a man can do and actually does, it matters little what he chooses to profess. If Herr Joachim thinks it expedient to profess that he has developed his fine style in the company of Herr Hiller, or of R. Schumann, this may rest upon its merits, provided he always plays in such wise that one may recognise the good results of several years intimate intercourse with Liszt. I also think it an advantage that when a "High-School of Music" was first thought of, the promoters at once secured the services of an admirable *practical master of style and execution.* If, to-day, I had to put a theatre capellmeister in the way of comprehending how he ought to conduct a piece, I would much rather refer him to Frau *Lucca,* than to the late Cantor *Hauptmann* at Leipzig, even if the latter were still alive. In this point I agree with the naïve portion of the public, and indeed, with the taste of the aristocratic patrons of the opera, for I prefer to deal with persons who actually bring forth something that appeals to the ear and to the feelings. Yet, I cannot help entertaining some little doubt, when I see Herr Joachim—all alone and solitary—sitting on high in the curule chair of the Academy—with nothing in his hand but a violin; for towards violinists generally I have always felt as Mephistopheles feels towards "the fair," whom he affects "once for all in the plural." The conductor's *baton* is reported not to have worked well in Herr Joachim's hands; composition, too, appears rather to have been a source of bitterness to him than of pleasure to others. I fail to see how "the high-school" is to be directed solely from the "high-stool" of the violinist. Socrates, at least, was not of opinion that Themistocles, Cimon and Pericles would prove capable of guiding the State by reason of their abilities as commanders and speakers; for, unfortunately, he could point to the results of their successes, and shew that the administration of State affairs became a source of personal trouble to them. But perhaps the case is different in the realms of music.

Yet another thing appears dubious. I am told that Herr J. Brahms expects all possible good to result from a return to the melody of Schubert's songs, and that Herr Joachim, for his own part, expects a *new Messiah* for music in general. Ought he not to leave such expectations to those who have chosen him " high-schoolmaster ? " I, for my part, say to him " Go in, and win ! " If it should come to pass that he himself is the Messiah, he may, at all events, rest assured that the Jews will not crucify him.

FINIS

APPENDIX.

APPENDIX   A.

BERICHT an Seine Majestät den König Ludwig II., von Bayern über eine in München zu errichtende Deutsche Musik-schule. (Report concerning a German music-school to be established at Munich) 1865. Reprinted in Wagner's "*Gesammelte Schriften*," Vol. VIII., p. 159-219, Leipzig, 1873.

p. 20. . . "We possess classical works, but we are not in possession of a classical style for the execution of these works." . . . "Does Germany possess a school at which the proper execution of Mozart's music is taught? Or do our orchestras and their conductors manage to play Mozart in accordance with some occult knowledge of their own? If so, whence do they derive such knowledge? Who taught it them? Take the simplest examples, Mozart's instrumental pieces (by no means his most important works, for these belong to the operatic stage), two things are at once apparent: the melodies must be beautifully *sung*; yet there are very few marks in the scores to shew *how* they are to be sung. It is well known that Mozart wrote the scores of his symphonies hurriedly,

in most cases simply for the purpose of performance
at some concert he was about to give; on the other
hand, it is also well known that he made great demands
upon the orchestra in the matter of expression.
Obviously he trusted to his personal influence over the
musicians. In the orchestra parts it was thus sufficient
to note the main *tempo* and piano or forte for entire
periods, since the master, who conducted the
rehearsals, could give spoken directions as to details,
and, by singing his themes, communicate the proper
expression to the players.

We are, now-a-days, accustomed to mark all details
of expression in the parts; nevertheless an intelligent
conductor frequently finds it expedient to indicate
important but very delicate *nuances* of expression by
word of mouth to the particular musicians whom they
concern; and, as a rule, such spoken directions are
better understood and attended to than the written
signs. It is obvious that in the rendering of Mozart's
instrumental music spoken directions played an
important part. With Mozart the so-called development sections, and the connecting links between the
main themes, are frequently rather slight, whereas his
musical originality shows to greatest advantage in the
vocal character of the melodies. Compared with Haydn's
the significance of Mozart's symphonies lies in the
extraordinarily expressive vocal character of his instrumental themes. Now, had Germany been in possession
of an authoritative institution, like the Conservatoire of
Paris, and had Mozart been asked to assist in the execu-

tion of his works, and to superintend the spirit of the
performances at such an institution, we might possibly
have something like an authoritative tradition amongst
us—a tradition such as, in spite of decay and corruption,
is still surprisingly vivid at the Paris Conservatoire—for
instance, in the case of Gluck's operas. But nothing of
the sort exists with us.   Mozart, as a rule, wrote a
symphony for some special concert, performed it once,
with an orchestra casually engaged, at Vienna, Prague,
or Leipzig ; and the traditions of such casual performances are completely lost.

No trace is preserved, except the scantily-marked
scores. And these classical relics of a once warmly
vibrating work are now accepted, with mistaken trust,
as the sole guide towards a new living performance.
Now, let us imagine such an expressive theme of
Mozart's—Mozart, who was intimately acquainted with
the noble style of classical Italian singing, whose
musical expression derived its very soul from the
delicate vibrations, swellings and accents of that style,
and who was the first to reproduce the effects of this
vocal style, by means of orchestral instruments—let us
imagine such a theme of the Master's played neatly
and smoothly, by an instrument in the orchestra,
without any inflection, or increase or decrease of tone
and accent, without the slightest touch of that modification of movement and rhythm so indispensable to
good singing—but monotonously enunciated, just as one
might pronounce some arithmetical number—and then,
let us endeavour to form a conclusion as to the vast

difference between the master's original intention, and
the impression thus produced. The dubious value of
the veneration for Mozart, professed by our music-
conservators, will then also appear. To show this
more distinctly, let us examine a particular case—for
example, the first eight bars of the second movement
of Mozart's celebrated symphony in E flat. Take this
beautiful theme as it appears on paper, with hardly
any marks of expression—fancy it played smoothly and
complacently, as the score apparently has it—and
compare the result with the manner in which a true
musician would feel and sing it ! How much of Mozart
does the theme convey, if played, as in nine cases out
of ten it *is* played, in a perfectly colourless and lifeless
way ? " Poor pen and paper music, without a shadow
of soul or sense."   (Eine seelenlose Schriftmusik).

APPENDIX B.

See p. 62, *et seq.* of Wagner's "*Beethoven,*" translated by E Dannreuther, London, 1882.

" A BEETHOVEN DAY : " *Beethoven's string quartet in C sharp minor.* " If we rest content to recall the tone-poem to memory, an attempt at illustration such as the following may perhaps prove possible, at least up to a certain degree ; whereas it would hardly be feasible during an actual performance. For, whilst listening to the work, we are bound to eschew any definite comparisons, being solely conscious of an immediate revelation from another world. Even then, however, the animation of the picture, in its several details, has to be left to the reader's fancy, and an outline sketch must therefore suffice. The longer introductory Adagio, than which probably nothing more melancholy has been expressed in tones, I would designate as the awakening on the morn of a day that throughout its tardy course shall fulfil not a single desire: not one.* None the less it is a penitential prayer,

---

* " Den Tag zu sehen, der mir in seinem Lauf
  Nicht einen Wunsch erfüllen wird, nicht Einen."
                                                            Faust.

a conterence with God in the faith of the eternally good. The eye turned inwards here, too, sees the comforting phenomena it alone can perceive (Allegro $\frac{6}{8}$), in which the longing becomes a sweet, tender, melancholy disport with itself;* the inmost hidden dream-picture awakens as the loveliest reminiscence. And now, in the short transitional *Allegro moderato* it is as though the Master, conscious of his strength, puts himself in position to work his spells; with renewed power he now practises his magic (Andante $\frac{2}{4}$), in banning a lovely figure, the witness of pure heavenly innocence, so that he may incessantly enrapture himself by its ever new and unheard of transformations, induced by the refraction of the rays of light he casts upon it. We may now (Presto $\frac{2}{2}$) fancy him, profoundly happy from within, casting an inexpressibly serene glance upon the outer world; and, again, it stands before him as in the Pastoral Symphony. Everything is luminous, reflecting his inner happiness; It is as though he were listening to the very tones emitted by the phenomena, that move, aerial and again firm, in rhythmical dance before him. He contemplates Life, and appears to reflect how he is to play a dance for Life itself (Short Adagio $\frac{3}{4}$); a short, but troubled meditation—as though he were diving into the soul's deep dream. He has again caught sight of the inner side of the world; he wakens and strikes the strings for a dance, such as the world has

---

* Ein wehmüthig holdes Spiel.

never heard (Allegro Finale). It is the World's own dance ; wild delight, cries of anguish, love's ecstacy, highest rapture, misery, rage ; voluptuous now, and sorrowful ; lightnings quiver, storm's roll ; and high above the gigantic musician ! banning and compelling all things, proudly and firmly wielding them from whirl to whirlpool, to the abyss.—He laughs at himself; for the incantation was, after all, but play to him. Thus night beckons. His day is done.

It is not possible to consider the man, Beethoven, in any sort of light, without at once having recourse to the wonderful musician, by way of elucidation.

APPENDIX C.

See p. 24 of *"Bericht,"* and "Wagner, Ges. Schriften," Vol. VIII., p. 186.

" IT IS difficult to understand Bach's music without a special musical and intellectual training, and it is a mistake to present it to the public in the careless and shallow modern way we have grown accustomed to. Those who so present it show that they do not know what they are about. . . . . The proper execution of Bach's music implies the solution of a difficult problem.   Tradition, even if it could be shown to exist in a definite form, offers little assistance ; for Bach, like every other German master, never had the means at his command adequately to perform his compositions. We know the embarrassing circumstances under which his most difficult and elaborate works were given—and it is not surprising that in the end he should have grown callous with regard to execution, and have considered his works as existing merely in thought. It is a task reserved for the highest and most comprehensive musical culture, to discover and establish a mode of executing the works of this wonderful master, so as to enable his music to appeal to the emotions in a plain direct manner.

APPENDIX D.

See Sir George Grove's "Dictionary of Music and Musicians." Vol. IV., p. 369. Article "Wagner."

"IN early days I thought more would come of Schumann. His *Zeitschrift* was brilliant and his pianoforte works showed great originality. There was much ferment, but also much real power, and many bits are quite unique and perfect. I think highly, too, of many of his songs, though they are not as great as Schubert's. He took pains with his declamation—no small merit forty years ago. Later on I saw a good deal of him at Dresden; but then already his head was tired, his powers on the wane. He consulted me about the text to his opera,'Genoveva,' which he was arranging from Tieck's and Hebbel's plays, yet he would not take my advice—he seemed to fear some trick."

A CATALOG OF SELECTED
DOVER BOOKS
IN ALL FIELDS OF INTEREST

A CATALOG OF SELECTED DOVER
BOOKS IN ALL FIELDS OF INTEREST

CONCERNING THE SPIRITUAL IN ART, Wassily Kandinsky. Pioneering work by father of abstract art. Thoughts on color theory, nature of art. Analysis of earlier masters. 12 illustrations. 80pp. of text. 5⅜ x 8½.   23411-8 Pa. $4.95

ANIMALS: 1,419 Copyright-Free Illustrations of Mammals, Birds, Fish, Insects, etc., Jim Harter (ed.). Clear wood engravings present, in extremely lifelike poses, over 1,000 species of animals. One of the most extensive pictorial sourcebooks of its kind. Captions. Index. 284pp. 9 x 12.   23766-4 Pa. $14.95

CELTIC ART: The Methods of Construction, George Bain. Simple geometric techniques for making Celtic interlacements, spirals, Kells-type initials, animals, humans, etc. Over 500 illustrations. 160pp. 9 x 12. (Available in U.S. only.)   22923-8 Pa. $9.95

AN ATLAS OF ANATOMY FOR ARTISTS, Fritz Schider. Most thorough reference work on art anatomy in the world. Hundreds of illustrations, including selections from works by Vesalius, Leonardo, Goya, Ingres, Michelangelo, others. 593 illustrations. 192pp. 7⅛ x 10¼.   20241-0 Pa. $9.95

CELTIC HAND STROKE-BY-STROKE (Irish Half-Uncial from "The Book of Kells"): An Arthur Baker Calligraphy Manual, Arthur Baker. Complete guide to creating each letter of the alphabet in distinctive Celtic manner. Covers hand position, strokes, pens, inks, paper, more. Illustrated. 48pp. 8¼ x 11.   24336-2 Pa. $3.95

EASY ORIGAMI, John Montroll. Charming collection of 32 projects (hat, cup, pelican, piano, swan, many more) specially designed for the novice origami hobbyist. Clearly illustrated easy-to-follow instructions insure that even beginning papercrafters will achieve successful results. 48pp. 8¼ x 11.   27298-2 Pa. $3.50

THE COMPLETE BOOK OF BIRDHOUSE CONSTRUCTION FOR WOODWORKERS, Scott D. Campbell. Detailed instructions, illustrations, tables. Also data on bird habitat and instinct patterns. Bibliography. 3 tables. 63 illustrations in 15 figures. 48pp. 5¼ x 8½.   24407-5 Pa. $2.50

BLOOMINGDALE'S ILLUSTRATED 1886 CATALOG: Fashions, Dry Goods and Housewares, Bloomingdale Brothers. Famed merchants' extremely rare catalog depicting about 1,700 products: clothing, housewares, firearms, dry goods, jewelry, more. Invaluable for dating, identifying vintage items. Also, copyright-free graphics for artists, designers. Co-published with Henry Ford Museum & Greenfield Village. 160pp. 8¼ x 11.   25780-0 Pa. $12.95

HISTORIC COSTUME IN PICTURES, Braun & Schneider. Over 1,450 costumed figures in clearly detailed engravings–from dawn of civilization to end of 19th century. Captions. Many folk costumes. 256pp. 8⅜ x 11¾.   23150-X Pa. $12.95

STICKLEY CRAFTSMAN FURNITURE CATALOGS, Gustav Stickley and L. & J. G. Stickley. Beautiful, functional furniture in two authentic catalogs from 1910. 594 illustrations, including 277 photos, show settles, rockers, armchairs, reclining chairs, bookcases, desks, tables. 183pp. 6½ x 9¼. 23838-5 Pa. $11.95

AMERICAN LOCOMOTIVES IN HISTORIC PHOTOGRAPHS: 1858 to 1949, Ron Ziel (ed.). A rare collection of 126 meticulously detailed official photographs, called "builder portraits," of American locomotives that majestically chronicle the rise of steam locomotive power in America. Introduction. Detailed captions. xi+ 129pp. 9 x 12. 27393-8 Pa. $13.95

AMERICA'S LIGHTHOUSES: An Illustrated History, Francis Ross Holland, Jr. Delightfully written, profusely illustrated fact-filled survey of over 200 American lighthouses since 1716. History, anecdotes, technological advances, more. 240pp. 8 x 10¾. 25576-X Pa. $12.95

TOWARDS A NEW ARCHITECTURE, Le Corbusier. Pioneering manifesto by founder of "International School." Technical and aesthetic theories, views of industry, economics, relation of form to function, "mass-production split" and much more. Profusely illustrated. 320pp. 6⅛ x 9¼. (Available in U.S. only.) 25023-7 Pa. $10.95

HOW THE OTHER HALF LIVES, Jacob Riis. Famous journalistic record, exposing poverty and degradation of New York slums around 1900, by major social reformer. 100 striking and influential photographs. 233pp. 10 x 7⅞. 22012-5 Pa. $11.95

FRUIT KEY AND TWIG KEY TO TREES AND SHRUBS, William M. Harlow. One of the handiest and most widely used identification aids. Fruit key covers 120 deciduous and evergreen species; twig key 160 deciduous species. Easily used. Over 300 photographs. 126pp. 5⅜ x 8½. 20511-8 Pa. $3.95

COMMON BIRD SONGS, Dr. Donald J. Borror. Songs of 60 most common U.S. birds: robins, sparrows, cardinals, bluejays, finches, more–arranged in order of increasing complexity. Up to 9 variations of songs of each species. Cassette and manual 99911-4 $8.95

ORCHIDS AS HOUSE PLANTS, Rebecca Tyson Northen. Grow cattleyas and many other kinds of orchids–in a window, in a case, or under artificial light. 63 illustrations. 148pp. 5⅜ x 8½. 23261-1 Pa. $7.95

MONSTER MAZES, Dave Phillips. Masterful mazes at four levels of difficulty. Avoid deadly perils and evil creatures to find magical treasures. Solutions for all 32 exciting illustrated puzzles. 48pp. 8¼ x 11. 26005-4 Pa. $2.95

MOZART'S DON GIOVANNI (DOVER OPERA LIBRETTO SERIES), Wolfgang Amadeus Mozart. Introduced and translated by Ellen H. Bleiler. Standard Italian libretto, with complete English translation. Convenient and thoroughly portable–an ideal companion for reading along with a recording or the performance itself. Introduction. List of characters. Plot summary. 121pp. 5¼ x 8½. 24944-1 Pa. $3.95

TECHNICAL MANUAL AND DICTIONARY OF CLASSICAL BALLET, Gail Grant. Defines, explains, comments on steps, movements, poses and concepts. 15-page pictorial section. Basic book for student, viewer. 127pp. 5⅜ x 8½. 21843-0 Pa. $4.95

THE CLARINET AND CLARINET PLAYING, David Pino. Lively, comprehensive work features suggestions about technique, musicianship, and musical interpretation, as well as guidelines for teaching, making your own reeds, and preparing for public performance. Includes an intriguing look at clarinet history. "A godsend," *The Clarinet,* Journal of the International Clarinet Society. Appendixes. 7 illus. 320pp. 5⅜ x 8½. 40270-3 Pa. $9.95

HOLLYWOOD GLAMOR PORTRAITS, John Kobal (ed.). 145 photos from 1926-49. Harlow, Gable, Bogart, Bacall; 94 stars in all. Full background on photographers, technical aspects. 160pp. 8⅜ x 11¼. 23352-9 Pa. $12.95

THE ANNOTATED CASEY AT THE BAT: A Collection of Ballads about the Mighty Casey/Third, Revised Edition, Martin Gardner (ed.). Amusing sequels and parodies of one of America's best-loved poems: Casey's Revenge, Why Casey Whiffed, Casey's Sister at the Bat, others. 256pp. 5⅜ x 8½. 28598-7 Pa. $8.95

THE RAVEN AND OTHER FAVORITE POEMS, Edgar Allan Poe. Over 40 of the author's most memorable poems: "The Bells," "Ulalume," "Israfel," "To Helen," "The Conqueror Worm," "Eldorado," "Annabel Lee," many more. Alphabetic lists of titles and first lines. 64pp. 5$\frac{3}{16}$ x 8¼. 26685-0 Pa. $1.00

PERSONAL MEMOIRS OF U. S. GRANT, Ulysses Simpson Grant. Intelligent, deeply moving firsthand account of Civil War campaigns, considered by many the finest military memoirs ever written. Includes letters, historic photographs, maps and more. 528pp. 6⅛ x 9¼. 28587-1 Pa. $12.95

ANCIENT EGYPTIAN MATERIALS AND INDUSTRIES, A. Lucas and J. Harris. Fascinating, comprehensive, thoroughly documented text describes this ancient civilization's vast resources and the processes that incorporated them in daily life, including the use of animal products, building materials, cosmetics, perfumes and incense, fibers, glazed ware, glass and its manufacture, materials used in the mummification process, and much more. 544pp. 6⅛ x 9¼. (Available in U.S. only.) 40446-3 Pa. $16.95

RUSSIAN STORIES/PYCCKNE PACCKA3bl: A Dual-Language Book, edited by Gleb Struve. Twelve tales by such masters as Chekhov, Tolstoy, Dostoevsky, Pushkin, others. Excellent word-for-word English translations on facing pages, plus teaching and study aids, Russian/English vocabulary, biographical/critical introductions, more. 416pp. 5⅜ x 8½. 26244-8 Pa. $9.95

PHILADELPHIA THEN AND NOW: 60 Sites Photographed in the Past and Present, Kenneth Finkel and Susan Oyama. Rare photographs of City Hall, Logan Square, Independence Hall, Betsy Ross House, other landmarks juxtaposed with contemporary views. Captures changing face of historic city. Introduction. Captions. 128pp. 8¼ x 11. 25790-8 Pa. $9.95

AIA ARCHITECTURAL GUIDE TO NASSAU AND SUFFOLK COUNTIES, LONG ISLAND, The American Institute of Architects, Long Island Chapter, and the Society for the Preservation of Long Island Antiquities. Comprehensive, well-researched and generously illustrated volume brings to life over three centuries of Long Island's great architectural heritage. More than 240 photographs with authoritative, extensively detailed captions. 176pp. 8¼ x 11. 26946-9 Pa. $14.95

NORTH AMERICAN INDIAN LIFE: Customs and Traditions of 23 Tribes, Elsie Clews Parsons (ed.). 27 fictionalized essays by noted anthropologists examine religion, customs, government, additional facets of life among the Winnebago, Crow, Zuni, Eskimo, other tribes. 480pp. 6⅛ x 9¼. 27377-6 Pa. $10.95

FRANK LLOYD WRIGHT'S DANA HOUSE, Donald Hoffmann. Pictorial essay of residential masterpiece with over 160 interior and exterior photos, plans, elevations, sketches and studies. 128pp. 9¼ x 10¾. 29120-0 Pa. $14.95

THE MALE AND FEMALE FIGURE IN MOTION: 60 Classic Photographic Sequences, Eadweard Muybridge. 60 true-action photographs of men and women walking, running, climbing, bending, turning, etc., reproduced from rare 19th-century masterpiece. vi + 121pp. 9 x 12. 24745-7 Pa. $12.95

1001 QUESTIONS ANSWERED ABOUT THE SEASHORE, N. J. Berrill and Jacquelyn Berrill. Queries answered about dolphins, sea snails, sponges, starfish, fishes, shore birds, many others. Covers appearance, breeding, growth, feeding, much more. 305pp. 5¼ x 8¼. 23366-9 Pa. $9.95

ATTRACTING BIRDS TO YOUR YARD, William J. Weber. Easy-to-follow guide offers advice on how to attract the greatest diversity of birds: birdhouses, feeders, water and waterers, much more. 96pp. $5\frac{3}{16}$ x 8¼. 28927-3 Pa. $2.50

MEDICINAL AND OTHER USES OF NORTH AMERICAN PLANTS: A Historical Survey with Special Reference to the Eastern Indian Tribes, Charlotte Erichsen-Brown. Chronological historical citations document 500 years of usage of plants, trees, shrubs native to eastern Canada, northeastern U.S. Also complete identifying information. 343 illustrations. 544pp. 6½ x 9¼. 25951-X Pa. $12.95

STORYBOOK MAZES, Dave Phillips. 23 stories and mazes on two-page spreads: Wizard of Oz, Treasure Island, Robin Hood, etc. Solutions. 64pp. 8¼ x 11. 23628-5 Pa. $2.95

AMERICAN NEGRO SONGS: 230 Folk Songs and Spirituals, Religious and Secular, John W. Work. This authoritative study traces the African influences of songs sung and played by black Americans at work, in church, and as entertainment. The author discusses the lyric significance of such songs as "Swing Low, Sweet Chariot," "John Henry," and others and offers the words and music for 230 songs. Bibliography. Index of Song Titles. 272pp. 6½ x 9¼. 40271-1 Pa. $10.95

MOVIE-STAR PORTRAITS OF THE FORTIES, John Kobal (ed.). 163 glamor, studio photos of 106 stars of the 1940s: Rita Hayworth, Ava Gardner, Marlon Brando, Clark Gable, many more. 176pp. 8⅜ x 11¼. 23546-7 Pa. $14.95

BENCHLEY LOST AND FOUND, Robert Benchley. Finest humor from early 30s, about pet peeves, child psychologists, post office and others. Mostly unavailable elsewhere. 73 illustrations by Peter Arno and others. 183pp. 5⅜ x 8½. 22410-4 Pa. $6.95

YEKL and THE IMPORTED BRIDEGROOM AND OTHER STORIES OF YIDDISH NEW YORK, Abraham Cahan. Film Hester Street based on *Yekl* (1896). Novel, other stories among first about Jewish immigrants on N.Y.'s East Side. 240pp. 5⅜ x 8½. 22427-9 Pa. $7.95

SELECTED POEMS, Walt Whitman. Generous sampling from *Leaves of Grass*. Twenty-four poems include "I Hear America Singing," "Song of the Open Road," "I Sing the Body Electric," "When Lilacs Last in the Dooryard Bloom'd," "O Captain! My Captain!"–all reprinted from an authoritative edition. Lists of titles and first lines. 128pp. $5\frac{3}{16}$ x 8¼. 26878-0 Pa. $1.00

THE BEST TALES OF HOFFMANN, E. T. A. Hoffmann. 10 of Hoffmann's most important stories: "Nutcracker and the King of Mice," "The Golden Flowerpot," etc. 458pp. 5⅜ x 8½. 21793-0 Pa. $9.95

FROM FETISH TO GOD IN ANCIENT EGYPT, E. A. Wallis Budge. Rich detailed survey of Egyptian conception of "God" and gods, magic, cult of animals, Osiris, more. Also, superb English translations of hymns and legends. 240 illustrations. 545pp. 5⅜ x 8½. 25803-3 Pa. $13.95

FRENCH STORIES/CONTES FRANÇAIS: A Dual-Language Book, Wallace Fowlie. Ten stories by French masters, Voltaire to Camus: "Micromegas" by Voltaire; "The Atheist's Mass" by Balzac; "Minuet" by de Maupassant; "The Guest" by Camus, six more. Excellent English translations on facing pages. Also French-English vocabulary list, exercises, more. 352pp. 5⅜ x 8½. 26443-2 Pa. $9.95

CHICAGO AT THE TURN OF THE CENTURY IN PHOTOGRAPHS: 122 Historic Views from the Collections of the Chicago Historical Society, Larry A. Viskochil. Rare large-format prints offer detailed views of City Hall, State Street, the Loop, Hull House, Union Station, many other landmarks, circa 1904-1913. Introduction. Captions. Maps. 144pp. 9⅜ x 12¼. 24656-6 Pa. $12.95

OLD BROOKLYN IN EARLY PHOTOGRAPHS, 1865-1929, William Lee Younger. Luna Park, Gravesend race track, construction of Grand Army Plaza, moving of Hotel Brighton, etc. 157 previously unpublished photographs. 165pp. 8⅞ x 11¾. 23587-4 Pa. $13.95

THE MYTHS OF THE NORTH AMERICAN INDIANS, Lewis Spence. Rich anthology of the myths and legends of the Algonquins, Iroquois, Pawnees and Sioux, prefaced by an extensive historical and ethnological commentary. 36 illustrations. 480pp. 5⅜ x 8½. 25967-6 Pa. $10.95

AN ENCYCLOPEDIA OF BATTLES: Accounts of Over 1,560 Battles from 1479 B.C. to the Present, David Eggenberger. Essential details of every major battle in recorded history from the first battle of Megiddo in 1479 B.C. to Grenada in 1984. List of Battle Maps. New Appendix covering the years 1967-1984. Index. 99 illustrations. 544pp. 6½ x 9¼. 24913-1 Pa. $16.95

SAILING ALONE AROUND THE WORLD, Captain Joshua Slocum. First man to sail around the world, alone, in small boat. One of great feats of seamanship told in delightful manner. 67 illustrations. 294pp. 5⅜ x 8½. 20326-3 Pa. $6.95

ANARCHISM AND OTHER ESSAYS, Emma Goldman. Powerful, penetrating, prophetic essays on direct action, role of minorities, prison reform, puritan hypocrisy, violence, etc. 271pp. 5⅜ x 8½. 22484-8 Pa. $8.95

MYTHS OF THE HINDUS AND BUDDHISTS, Ananda K. Coomaraswamy and Sister Nivedita. Great stories of the epics; deeds of Krishna, Shiva, taken from puranas, Vedas, folk tales; etc. 32 illustrations. 400pp. 5⅜ x 8½. 21759-0 Pa. $12.95

THE TRAUMA OF BIRTH, Otto Rank. Rank's controversial thesis that anxiety neurosis is caused by profound psychological trauma which occurs at birth. 256pp. 5⅜ x 8½. 27974-X Pa. $7.95

A THEOLOGICO-POLITICAL TREATISE, Benedict Spinoza. Also contains unfinished Political Treatise. Great classic on religious liberty, theory of government on common consent. R. Elwes translation. Total of 421pp. 5⅜ x 8½. 20249-6 Pa. $10.95

MY BONDAGE AND MY FREEDOM, Frederick Douglass. Born a slave, Douglass became outspoken force in antislavery movement. The best of Douglass' autobiographies. Graphic description of slave life. 464pp. 5⅜ x 8½. 22457-0 Pa. $8.95

FOLLOWING THE EQUATOR: A Journey Around the World, Mark Twain. Fascinating humorous account of 1897 voyage to Hawaii, Australia, India, New Zealand, etc. Ironic, bemused reports on peoples, customs, climate, flora and fauna, politics, much more. 197 illustrations. 720pp. 5⅜ x 8½. 26113-1 Pa. $15.95

THE PEOPLE CALLED SHAKERS, Edward D. Andrews. Definitive study of Shakers: origins, beliefs, practices, dances, social organization, furniture and crafts, etc. 33 illustrations. 351pp. 5⅜ x 8½. 21081-2 Pa. $12.95

THE MYTHS OF GREECE AND ROME, H. A. Guerber. A classic of mythology, generously illustrated, long prized for its simple, graphic, accurate retelling of the principal myths of Greece and Rome, and for its commentary on their origins and significance. With 64 illustrations by Michelangelo, Raphael, Titian, Rubens, Canova, Bernini and others. 480pp. 5⅜ x 8½. 27584-1 Pa. $10.95

PSYCHOLOGY OF MUSIC, Carl E. Seashore. Classic work discusses music as a medium from psychological viewpoint. Clear treatment of physical acoustics, auditory apparatus, sound perception, development of musical skills, nature of musical feeling, host of other topics. 88 figures. 408pp. 5⅜ x 8½. 21851-1 Pa. $11.95

THE PHILOSOPHY OF HISTORY, Georg W. Hegel. Great classic of Western thought develops concept that history is not chance but rational process, the evolution of freedom. 457pp. 5⅜ x 8½. 20112-0 Pa. $9.95

THE BOOK OF TEA, Kakuzo Okakura. Minor classic of the Orient: entertaining, charming explanation, interpretation of traditional Japanese culture in terms of tea ceremony. 94pp. 5⅜ x 8½. 20070-1 Pa. $3.95

LIFE IN ANCIENT EGYPT, Adolf Erman. Fullest, most thorough, detailed older account with much not in more recent books, domestic life, religion, magic, medicine, commerce, much more. Many illustrations reproduce tomb paintings, carvings, hieroglyphs, etc. 597pp. 5⅜ x 8½. 22632-8 Pa. $12.95

SUNDIALS, Their Theory and Construction, Albert Waugh. Far and away the best, most thorough coverage of ideas, mathematics concerned, types, construction, adjusting anywhere. Simple, nontechnical treatment allows even children to build several of these dials. Over 100 illustrations. 230pp. 5⅜ x 8½. 22947-5 Pa. $8.95

THEORETICAL HYDRODYNAMICS, L. M. Milne-Thomson. Classic exposition of the mathematical theory of fluid motion, applicable to both hydrodynamics and aerodynamics. Over 600 exercises. 768pp. 6⅛ x 9¼. 68970-0 Pa. $20.95

SONGS OF EXPERIENCE: Facsimile Reproduction with 26 Plates in Full Color, William Blake. 26 full-color plates from a rare 1826 edition. Includes "TheTyger," "London," "Holy Thursday," and other poems. Printed text of poems. 48pp. 5¼ x 7. 24636-1 Pa. $4.95

OLD-TIME VIGNETTES IN FULL COLOR, Carol Belanger Grafton (ed.). Over 390 charming, often sentimental illustrations, selected from archives of Victorian graphics—pretty women posing, children playing, food, flowers, kittens and puppies, smiling cherubs, birds and butterflies, much more. All copyright-free. 48pp. 9¼ x 12¼. 27269-9 Pa. $9.95

PERSPECTIVE FOR ARTISTS, Rex Vicat Cole. Depth, perspective of sky and sea, shadows, much more, not usually covered. 391 diagrams, 81 reproductions of drawings and paintings. 279pp. 5⅜ x 8½. 22487-2 Pa. $9.95

DRAWING THE LIVING FIGURE, Joseph Sheppard. Innovative approach to artistic anatomy focuses on specifics of surface anatomy, rather than muscles and bones. Over 170 drawings of live models in front, back and side views, and in widely varying poses. Accompanying diagrams. 177 illustrations. Introduction. Index. 144pp. 8⅜ x11¼. 26723-7 Pa. $9.95

GOTHIC AND OLD ENGLISH ALPHABETS: 100 Complete Fonts, Dan X. Solo. Add power, elegance to posters, signs, other graphics with 100 stunning copyright-free alphabets: Blackstone, Dolbey, Germania, 97 more–including many lower-case, numerals, punctuation marks. 104pp. 8⅛ x 11. 24695-7 Pa. $9.95

HOW TO DO BEADWORK, Mary White. Fundamental book on craft from simple projects to five-bead chains and woven works. 106 illustrations. 142pp. 5⅜ x 8. 20697-1 Pa. $5.95

THE BOOK OF WOOD CARVING, Charles Marshall Sayers. Finest book for beginners discusses fundamentals and offers 34 designs. "Absolutely first rate . . . well thought out and well executed."–E. J. Tangerman. 118pp. 7¾ x 10⅝. 23654-4 Pa. $7.95

ILLUSTRATED CATALOG OF CIVIL WAR MILITARY GOODS: Union Army Weapons, Insignia, Uniform Accessories, and Other Equipment, Schuyler, Hartley, and Graham. Rare, profusely illustrated 1846 catalog includes Union Army uniform and dress regulations, arms and ammunition, coats, insignia, flags, swords, rifles, etc. 226 illustrations. 160pp. 9 x 12. 24939-5 Pa. $12.95

WOMEN'S FASHIONS OF THE EARLY 1900s: An Unabridged Republication of "New York Fashions, 1909," National Cloak & Suit Co. Rare catalog of mail-order fashions documents women's and children's clothing styles shortly after the turn of the century. Captions offer full descriptions, prices. Invaluable resource for fashion, costume historians. Approximately 725 illustrations. 128pp. 8⅜ x 11¼. 27276-1 Pa. $12.95

THE 1912 AND 1915 GUSTAV STICKLEY FURNITURE CATALOGS, Gustav Stickley. With over 200 detailed illustrations and descriptions, these two catalogs are essential reading and reference materials and identification guides for Stickley furniture. Captions cite materials, dimensions and prices. 112pp. 6½ x 9¼. 26676-1 Pa. $9.95

EARLY AMERICAN LOCOMOTIVES, John H. White, Jr. Finest locomotive engravings from early 19th century: historical (1804–74), main-line (after 1870), special, foreign, etc. 147 plates. 142pp. 11⅜ x 8¼. 22772-3 Pa. $12.95

THE TALL SHIPS OF TODAY IN PHOTOGRAPHS, Frank O. Braynard. Lavishly illustrated tribute to nearly 100 majestic contemporary sailing vessels: Amerigo Vespucci, Clearwater, Constitution, Eagle, Mayflower, Sea Cloud, Victory, many more. Authoritative captions provide statistics, background on each ship. 190 black-and-white photographs and illustrations. Introduction. 128pp. 8⅞ x 11¾. 27163-3 Pa. $14.95

LITTLE BOOK OF EARLY AMERICAN CRAFTS AND TRADES, Peter Stockham (ed.). 1807 children's book explains crafts and trades: baker, hatter, cooper, potter, and many others. 23 copperplate illustrations. 140pp. 4⅝ x 6.
23336-7 Pa. $4.95

VICTORIAN FASHIONS AND COSTUMES FROM HARPER'S BAZAR, 1867–1898, Stella Blum (ed.). Day costumes, evening wear, sports clothes, shoes, hats, other accessories in over 1,000 detailed engravings. 320pp. 9⅜ x 12¼.
22990-4 Pa. $16.95

GUSTAV STICKLEY, THE CRAFTSMAN, Mary Ann Smith. Superb study surveys broad scope of Stickley's achievement, especially in architecture. Design philosophy, rise and fall of the Craftsman empire, descriptions and floor plans for many Craftsman houses, more. 86 black-and-white halftones. 31 line illustrations. Introduction 208pp. 6½ x 9¼. 27210-9 Pa. $9.95

THE LONG ISLAND RAIL ROAD IN EARLY PHOTOGRAPHS, Ron Ziel. Over 220 rare photos, informative text document origin (1844) and development of rail service on Long Island. Vintage views of early trains, locomotives, stations, passengers, crews, much more. Captions. 8⅞ x 11¾. 26301-0 Pa. $14.95

VOYAGE OF THE LIBERDADE, Joshua Slocum. Great 19th-century mariner's thrilling, first-hand account of the wreck of his ship off South America, the 35-foot boat he built from the wreckage, and its remarkable voyage home. 128pp. 5⅜ x 8½.
40022-0 Pa. $5.95

TEN BOOKS ON ARCHITECTURE, Vitruvius. The most important book ever written on architecture. Early Roman aesthetics, technology, classical orders, site selection, all other aspects. Morgan translation. 331pp. 5⅜ x 8½. 20645-9 Pa. $9.95

THE HUMAN FIGURE IN MOTION, Eadweard Muybridge. More than 4,500 stopped-action photos, in action series, showing undraped men, women, children jumping, lying down, throwing, sitting, wrestling, carrying, etc. 390pp. 7⅞ x 10⅝.
20204-6 Clothbd. $29.95

TREES OF THE EASTERN AND CENTRAL UNITED STATES AND CANADA, William M. Harlow. Best one-volume guide to 140 trees. Full descriptions, woodlore, range, etc. Over 600 illustrations. Handy size. 288pp. 4½ x 6⅜.
20395-6 Pa. $6.95

SONGS OF WESTERN BIRDS, Dr. Donald J. Borror. Complete song and call repertoire of 60 western species, including flycatchers, juncoes, cactus wrens, many more–includes fully illustrated booklet. Cassette and manual 99913-0 $8.95

GROWING AND USING HERBS AND SPICES, Milo Miloradovich. Versatile handbook provides all the information needed for cultivation and use of all the herbs and spices available in North America. 4 illustrations. Index. Glossary. 236pp. 5⅜ x 8½.
25058-X Pa. $7.95

BIG BOOK OF MAZES AND LABYRINTHS, Walter Shepherd. 50 mazes and labyrinths in all–classical, solid, ripple, and more–in one great volume. Perfect inexpensive puzzler for clever youngsters. Full solutions. 112pp. 8⅛ x 11.
22951-3 Pa. $5.95

PIANO TUNING, J. Cree Fischer. Clearest, best book for beginner, amateur. Simple repairs, raising dropped notes, tuning by easy method of flattened fifths. No previous skills needed. 4 illustrations. 201pp. 5⅜ x 8½. 23267-0 Pa. $6.95

HINTS TO SINGERS, Lillian Nordica. Selecting the right teacher, developing confidence, overcoming stage fright, and many other important skills receive thoughtful discussion in this indispensible guide, written by a world-famous diva of four decades' experience. 96pp. 5⅜ x 8½. 40094-8 Pa. $4.95

THE COMPLETE NONSENSE OF EDWARD LEAR, Edward Lear. All nonsense limericks, zany alphabets, Owl and Pussycat, songs, nonsense botany, etc., illustrated by Lear. Total of 320pp. 5⅜ x 8½. (Available in U.S. only.) 20167-8 Pa. $7.95

VICTORIAN PARLOUR POETRY: An Annotated Anthology, Michael R. Turner. 117 gems by Longfellow, Tennyson, Browning, many lesser-known poets. "The Village Blacksmith," "Curfew Must Not Ring Tonight," "Only a Baby Small," dozens more, often difficult to find elsewhere. Index of poets, titles, first lines. xxiii + 325pp. 5⅝ x 8¼. 27044-0 Pa. $12.95

DUBLINERS, James Joyce. Fifteen stories offer vivid, tightly focused observations of the lives of Dublin's poorer classes. At least one, "The Dead," is considered a masterpiece. Reprinted complete and unabridged from standard edition. 160pp. 5³⁄₁₆ x 8¼. 26870-5 Pa. $1.50

GREAT WEIRD TALES: 14 Stories by Lovecraft, Blackwood, Machen and Others, S. T. Joshi (ed.). 14 spellbinding tales, including "The Sin Eater," by Fiona McLeod, "The Eye Above the Mantel," by Frank Belknap Long, as well as renowned works by R. H. Barlow, Lord Dunsany, Arthur Machen, W. C. Morrow and eight other masters of the genre. 256pp. 5⅜ x 8½. (Available in U.S. only.) 40436-6 Pa. $8.95

THE BOOK OF THE SACRED MAGIC OF ABRAMELIN THE MAGE, translated by S. MacGregor Mathers. Medieval manuscript of ceremonial magic. Basic document in Aleister Crowley, Golden Dawn groups. 268pp. 5⅜ x 8½. 23211-5 Pa. $9.95

NEW RUSSIAN-ENGLISH AND ENGLISH-RUSSIAN DICTIONARY, M. A. O'Brien. This is a remarkably handy Russian dictionary, containing a surprising amount of information, including over 70,000 entries. 366pp. 4½ x 6⅛. 20208-9 Pa. $10.95

HISTORIC HOMES OF THE AMERICAN PRESIDENTS, Second, Revised Edition, Irvin Haas. A traveler's guide to American Presidential homes, most open to the public, depicting and describing homes occupied by every American President from George Washington to George Bush. With visiting hours, admission charges, travel routes. 175 photographs. Index. 160pp. 8¼ x 11. 26751-2 Pa. $13.95

NEW YORK IN THE FORTIES, Andreas Feininger. 162 brilliant photographs by the well-known photographer, formerly with *Life* magazine. Commuters, shoppers, Times Square at night, much else from city at its peak. Captions by John von Hartz. 181pp. 9¼ x 10¾. 23585-8 Pa. $13.95

INDIAN SIGN LANGUAGE, William Tomkins. Over 525 signs developed by Sioux and other tribes. Written instructions and diagrams. Also 290 pictographs. 111pp. 6⅛ x 9¼. 22029-X Pa. $3.95

ANATOMY: A Complete Guide for Artists, Joseph Sheppard. A master of figure drawing shows artists how to render human anatomy convincingly. Over 460 illustrations. 224pp. 8⅜ x 11¼. 27279-6 Pa. $11.95

MEDIEVAL CALLIGRAPHY: Its History and Technique, Marc Drogin. Spirited history, comprehensive instruction manual covers 13 styles (ca. 4th century through 15th). Excellent photographs; directions for duplicating medieval techniques with modern tools. 224pp. 8⅜ x 11¼. 26142-5 Pa. $12.95

DRIED FLOWERS: How to Prepare Them, Sarah Whitlock and Martha Rankin. Complete instructions on how to use silica gel, meal and borax, perlite aggregate, sand and borax, glycerine and water to create attractive permanent flower arrangements. 12 illustrations. 32pp. 5⅜ x 8½. 21802-3 Pa. $1.00

EASY-TO-MAKE BIRD FEEDERS FOR WOODWORKERS, Scott D. Campbell. Detailed, simple-to-use guide for designing, constructing, caring for and using feeders. Text, illustrations for 12 classic and contemporary designs. 96pp. 5⅜ x 8½.
25847-5 Pa. $3.95

SCOTTISH WONDER TALES FROM MYTH AND LEGEND, Donald A. Mackenzie. 16 lively tales tell of giants rumbling down mountainsides, of a magic wand that turns stone pillars into warriors, of gods and goddesses, evil hags, powerful forces and more. 240pp. 5⅜ x 8½. 29677-6 Pa. $6.95

THE HISTORY OF UNDERCLOTHES, C. Willett Cunnington and Phyllis Cunnington. Fascinating, well-documented survey covering six centuries of English undergarments, enhanced with over 100 illustrations: 12th-century laced-up bodice, footed long drawers (1795), 19th-century bustles, l9th-century corsets for men, Victorian "bust improvers," much more. 272pp. 5⅜ x 8¼. 27124-2 Pa. $9.95

ARTS AND CRAFTS FURNITURE: The Complete Brooks Catalog of 1912, Brooks Manufacturing Co. Photos and detailed descriptions of more than 150 now very collectible furniture designs from the Arts and Crafts movement depict davenports, settees, buffets, desks, tables, chairs, bedsteads, dressers and more, all built of solid, quarter-sawed oak. Invaluable for students and enthusiasts of antiques, Americana and the decorative arts. 80pp. 6½ x 9¼. 27471-3 Pa. $8.95

WILBUR AND ORVILLE: A Biography of the Wright Brothers, Fred Howard. Definitive, crisply written study tells the full story of the brothers' lives and work. A vividly written biography, unparalleled in scope and color, that also captures the spirit of an extraordinary era. 560pp. 6⅛ x 9¼. 40297-5 Pa. $17.95

THE ARTS OF THE SAILOR: Knotting, Splicing and Ropework, Hervey Garrett Smith. Indispensable shipboard reference covers tools, basic knots and useful hitches; handsewing and canvas work, more. Over 100 illustrations. Delightful reading for sea lovers. 256pp. 5⅜ x 8½. 26440-8 Pa. $8.95

FRANK LLOYD WRIGHT'S FALLINGWATER: The House and Its History, Second, Revised Edition, Donald Hoffmann. A total revision—both in text and illustrations—of the standard document on Fallingwater, the boldest, most personal architectural statement of Wright's mature years, updated with valuable new material from the recently opened Frank Lloyd Wright Archives. "Fascinating"—*The New York Times*. 116 illustrations. 128pp. 9¼ x 10¾. 27430-6 Pa. $12.95

PHOTOGRAPHIC SKETCHBOOK OF THE CIVIL WAR, Alexander Gardner. 100 photos taken on field during the Civil War. Famous shots of Manassas Harper's Ferry, Lincoln, Richmond, slave pens, etc. 244pp. 10⅝ x 8¼.   22731-6 Pa. $10.95

FIVE ACRES AND INDEPENDENCE, Maurice G. Kains. Great back-to-the-land classic explains basics of self-sufficient farming. The one book to get. 95 illustrations. 397pp. 5⅜ x 8½.   20974-1 Pa. $7.95

SONGS OF EASTERN BIRDS, Dr. Donald J. Borror. Songs and calls of 60 species most common to eastern U.S.: warblers, woodpeckers, flycatchers, thrushes, larks, many more in high-quality recording.   Cassette and manual 99912-2 $9.95

A MODERN HERBAL, Margaret Grieve. Much the fullest, most exact, most useful compilation of herbal material. Gigantic alphabetical encyclopedia, from aconite to zedoary, gives botanical information, medical properties, folklore, economic uses, much else. Indispensable to serious reader. 161 illustrations. 888pp. 6½ x 9¼. 2-vol. set. (Available in U.S. only.)   Vol. I: 22798-7 Pa. $10.95
Vol. II: 22799-5 Pa. $10.95

HIDDEN TREASURE MAZE BOOK, Dave Phillips. Solve 34 challenging mazes accompanied by heroic tales of adventure. Evil dragons, people-eating plants, blood-thirsty giants, many more dangerous adversaries lurk at every twist and turn. 34 mazes, stories, solutions. 48pp. 8¼ x 11.   24566-7 Pa. $2.95

LETTERS OF W. A. MOZART, Wolfgang A. Mozart. Remarkable letters show bawdy wit, humor, imagination, musical insights, contemporary musical world; includes some letters from Leopold Mozart. 276pp. 5⅜ x 8½.   22859-2 Pa. $9.95

BASIC PRINCIPLES OF CLASSICAL BALLET, Agrippina Vaganova. Great Russian theoretician, teacher explains methods for teaching classical ballet. 118 illustrations. 175pp. 5⅜ x 8½.   22036-2 Pa. $6.95

THE JUMPING FROG, Mark Twain. Revenge edition. The original story of The Celebrated Jumping Frog of Calaveras County, a hapless French translation, and Twain's hilarious "retranslation" from the French. 12 illustrations. 66pp. 5⅜ x 8½.
22686-7 Pa. $4.95

BEST REMEMBERED POEMS, Martin Gardner (ed.). The 126 poems in this superb collection of 19th- and 20th-century British and American verse range from Shelley's "To a Skylark" to the impassioned "Renascence" of Edna St. Vincent Millay and to Edward Lear's whimsical "The Owl and the Pussycat." 224pp. 5⅜ x 8½.
27165-X Pa. $5.95

COMPLETE SONNETS, William Shakespeare. Over 150 exquisite poems deal with love, friendship, the tyranny of time, beauty's evanescence, death and other themes in language of remarkable power, precision and beauty. Glossary of archaic terms. 80pp. 5³⁄₁₆ x 8¼.   26686-9 Pa. $1.00

THE BATTLES THAT CHANGED HISTORY, Fletcher Pratt. Eminent historian profiles 16 crucial conflicts, ancient to modern, that changed the course of civilization. 352pp. 5⅜ x 8½.   41129-X Pa. $9.95

THE WIT AND HUMOR OF OSCAR WILDE, Alvin Redman (ed.). More than 1,000 ripostes, paradoxes, wisecracks: Work is the curse of the drinking classes; I can resist everything except temptation; etc. 258pp. 5⅜ x 8½. 20602-5 Pa. $6.95

SHAKESPEARE LEXICON AND QUOTATION DICTIONARY, Alexander Schmidt. Full definitions, locations, shades of meaning in every word in plays and poems. More than 50,000 exact quotations. 1,485pp. 6½ x 9¼. 2-vol. set.
Vol. 1: 22726-X Pa. $17.95
Vol. 2: 22727-8 Pa. $17.95

SELECTED POEMS, Emily Dickinson. Over 100 best-known, best-loved poems by one of America's foremost poets, reprinted from authoritative early editions. No comparable edition at this price. Index of first lines. 64pp. 5$\frac{3}{16}$ x 8¼.
26466-1 Pa. $1.00

THE INSIDIOUS DR. FU-MANCHU, Sax Rohmer. The first of the popular mystery series introduces a pair of English detectives to their archnemesis, the diabolical Dr. Fu-Manchu. Flavorful atmosphere, fast-paced action, and colorful characters enliven this classic of the genre. 208pp. 5$\frac{3}{16}$ x 8¼. 29898-1 Pa. $2.00

THE MALLEUS MALEFICARUM OF KRAMER AND SPRENGER, translated by Montague Summers. Full text of most important witchhunter's "bible," used by both Catholics and Protestants. 278pp. 6⅝ x 10. 22802-9 Pa. $12.95

SPANISH STORIES/CUENTOS ESPAÑOLES: A Dual-Language Book, Angel Flores (ed.). Unique format offers 13 great stories in Spanish by Cervantes, Borges, others. Faithful English translations on facing pages. 352pp. 5⅜ x 8½.
25399-6 Pa. $9.95

GARDEN CITY, LONG ISLAND, IN EARLY PHOTOGRAPHS, 1869–1919, Mildred H. Smith. Handsome treasury of 118 vintage pictures, accompanied by carefully researched captions, document the Garden City Hotel fire (1899), the Vanderbilt Cup Race (1908), the first airmail flight departing from the Nassau Boulevard Aerodrome (1911), and much more. 96pp. 8⅞ x 11¾. 40669-5 Pa. $12.95

OLD QUEENS, N.Y., IN EARLY PHOTOGRAPHS, Vincent F. Seyfried and William Asadorian. Over 160 rare photographs of Maspeth, Jamaica, Jackson Heights, and other areas. Vintage views of DeWitt Clinton mansion, 1939 World's Fair and more. Captions. 192pp. 8⅞ x 11. 26358-4 Pa. $14.95

CAPTURED BY THE INDIANS: 15 Firsthand Accounts, 1750-1870, Frederick Drimmer. Astounding true historical accounts of grisly torture, bloody conflicts, relentless pursuits, miraculous escapes and more, by people who lived to tell the tale. 384pp. 5⅜ x 8½. 24901-8 Pa. $9.95

THE WORLD'S GREAT SPEECHES (Fourth Enlarged Edition), Lewis Copeland, Lawrence W. Lamm, and Stephen J. McKenna. Nearly 300 speeches provide public speakers with a wealth of updated quotes and inspiration–from Pericles' funeral oration and William Jennings Bryan's "Cross of Gold Speech" to Malcolm X's powerful words on the Black Revolution and Earl of Spenser's tribute to his sister, Diana, Princess of Wales. 944pp. 5⅜ x 8⅜. 40903-1 Pa. $15.95

THE BOOK OF THE SWORD, Sir Richard F. Burton. Great Victorian scholar/adventurer's eloquent, erudite history of the "queen of weapons"–from prehistory to early Roman Empire. Evolution and development of early swords, variations (sabre, broadsword, cutlass, scimitar, etc.), much more. 336pp. 6⅛ x 9¼.
25434-8 Pa. $9.95

AUTOBIOGRAPHY: The Story of My Experiments with Truth, Mohandas K. Gandhi. Boyhood, legal studies, purification, the growth of the Satyagraha (nonviolent protest) movement. Critical, inspiring work of the man responsible for the freedom of India. 480pp. 5⅜ x 8½. (Available in U.S. only.) 24593-4 Pa. $9.95

CELTIC MYTHS AND LEGENDS, T. W. Rolleston. Masterful retelling of Irish and Welsh stories and tales. Cuchulain, King Arthur, Deirdre, the Grail, many more. First paperback edition. 58 full-page illustrations. 512pp. 5⅜ x 8½. 26507-2 Pa. $9.95

THE PRINCIPLES OF PSYCHOLOGY, William James. Famous long course complete, unabridged. Stream of thought, time perception, memory, experimental methods; great work decades ahead of its time. 94 figures. 1,391pp. 5⅜ x 8½. 2-vol. set.
Vol. I: 20381-6 Pa. $14.95
Vol. II: 20382-4 Pa. $16.95

THE WORLD AS WILL AND REPRESENTATION, Arthur Schopenhauer. Definitive English translation of Schopenhauer's life work, correcting more than 1,000 errors, omissions in earlier translations. Translated by E. F. J. Payne. Total of 1,269pp. 5⅜ x 8½. 2-vol. set.
Vol. 1: 21761-2 Pa. $12.95
Vol. 2: 21762-0 Pa. $12.95

MAGIC AND MYSTERY IN TIBET, Madame Alexandra David-Neel. Experiences among lamas, magicians, sages, sorcerers, Bonpa wizards. A true psychic discovery. 32 illustrations. 321pp. 5⅜ x 8½. (Available in U.S. only.) 22682-4 Pa. $9.95

THE EGYPTIAN BOOK OF THE DEAD, E. A. Wallis Budge. Complete reproduction of Ani's papyrus, finest ever found. Full hieroglyphic text, interlinear transliteration, word-for-word translation, smooth translation. 533pp. 6½ x 9¼.
21866-X Pa. $12.95

MATHEMATICS FOR THE NONMATHEMATICIAN, Morris Kline. Detailed, college-level treatment of mathematics in cultural and historical context, with numerous exercises. Recommended Reading Lists. Tables. Numerous figures. 641pp. 5⅜ x 8½.
24823-2 Pa. $11.95

PROBABILISTIC METHODS IN THE THEORY OF STRUCTURES, Isaac Elishakoff. Well-written introduction covers the elements of the theory of probability from two or more random variables, the reliability of such multivariable structures, the theory of random function, Monte Carlo methods of treating problems incapable of exact solution, and more. Examples. 502pp. 5³/₈ x 8¹/₂. 40691-1 Pa. $16.95

THE RIME OF THE ANCIENT MARINER, Gustave Doré, S. T. Coleridge. Doré's finest work; 34 plates capture moods, subtleties of poem. Flawless full-size reproductions printed on facing pages with authoritative text of poem. "Beautiful. Simply beautiful."–*Publisher's Weekly.* 77pp. 9¼ x 12. 22305-1 Pa. $7.95

NORTH AMERICAN INDIAN DESIGNS FOR ARTISTS AND CRAFTSPEOPLE, Eva Wilson. Over 360 authentic copyright-free designs adapted from Navajo blankets, Hopi pottery, Sioux buffalo hides, more. Geometrics, symbolic figures, plant and animal motifs, etc. 128pp. 8⅜ x 11. (Not for sale in the United Kingdom.) 25341-4 Pa. $9.95

SCULPTURE: Principles and Practice, Louis Slobodkin. Step-by-step approach to clay, plaster, metals, stone; classical and modern. 253 drawings, photos. 255pp. 8⅛ x 11.
22960-2 Pa. $11.95

THE INFLUENCE OF SEA POWER UPON HISTORY, 1660–1783, A. T. Mahan. Influential classic of naval history and tactics still used as text in war colleges. First paperback edition. 4 maps. 24 battle plans. 640pp. 5⅜ x 8½. 25509-3 Pa. $14.95

THE STORY OF THE TITANIC AS TOLD BY ITS SURVIVORS, Jack Winocour (ed.). What it was really like. Panic, despair, shocking inefficiency, and a little heroism. More thrilling than any fictional account. 26 illustrations. 320pp. 5⅜ x 8½. 20610-6 Pa. $8.95

FAIRY AND FOLK TALES OF THE IRISH PEASANTRY, William Butler Yeats (ed.). Treasury of 64 tales from the twilight world of Celtic myth and legend: "The Soul Cages," "The Kildare Pooka," "King O'Toole and his Goose," many more. Introduction and Notes by W. B. Yeats. 352pp. 5⅜ x 8½. 26941-8 Pa. $8.95

BUDDHIST MAHAYANA TEXTS, E. B. Cowell and others (eds.). Superb, accurate translations of basic documents in Mahayana Buddhism, highly important in history of religions. The Buddha-karita of Asvaghosha, Larger Sukhavativyuha, more. 448pp. 5⅜ x 8½. 25552-2 Pa. $12.95

ONE TWO THREE . . . INFINITY: Facts and Speculations of Science, George Gamow. Great physicist's fascinating, readable overview of contemporary science: number theory, relativity, fourth dimension, entropy, genes, atomic structure, much more. 128 illustrations. Index. 352pp. 5⅜ x 8½. 25664-2 Pa. $9.95

EXPERIMENTATION AND MEASUREMENT, W. J. Youden. Introductory manual explains laws of measurement in simple terms and offers tips for achieving accuracy and minimizing errors. Mathematics of measurement, use of instruments, experimenting with machines. 1994 edition. Foreword. Preface. Introduction. Epilogue. Selected Readings. Glossary. Index. Tables and figures. 128pp. 5⅜ x 8½. 40451-X Pa. $6.95

DALÍ ON MODERN ART: The Cuckolds of Antiquated Modern Art, Salvador Dalí. Influential painter skewers modern art and its practitioners. Outrageous evaluations of Picasso, Cézanne, Turner, more. 15 renderings of paintings discussed. 44 calligraphic decorations by Dalí. 96pp. 5⅜ x 8½. (Available in U.S. only.) 29220-7 Pa. $5.95

ANTIQUE PLAYING CARDS: A Pictorial History, Henry René D'Allemagne. Over 900 elaborate, decorative images from rare playing cards (14th–20th centuries): Bacchus, death, dancing dogs, hunting scenes, royal coats of arms, players cheating, much more. 96pp. 9¼ x 12¼. 29265-7 Pa. $12.95

MAKING FURNITURE MASTERPIECES: 30 Projects with Measured Drawings, Franklin H. Gottshall. Step-by-step instructions, illustrations for constructing handsome, useful pieces, among them a Sheraton desk, Chippendale chair, Spanish desk, Queen Anne table and a William and Mary dressing mirror. 224pp. 8⅛ x 11¼. 29338-6 Pa. $16.95

THE FOSSIL BOOK: A Record of Prehistoric Life, Patricia V. Rich et al. Profusely illustrated definitive guide covers everything from single-celled organisms and dinosaurs to birds and mammals and the interplay between climate and man. Over 1,500 illustrations. 760pp. 7½ x 10⅛. 29371-8 Pa. $29.95

Prices subject to change without notice.

Available at your book dealer or write for free catalog to Dept. GI, Dover Publications, Inc., 31 East 2nd St., Mineola, N.Y. 11501. Dover publishes more than 500 books each year on science, elementary and advanced mathematics, biology, music, art, literary history, social sciences and other areas.